APOSTASY

The Word-Faith Doctrinal Deception

Jeff Kluttz

Copyright © 2011, Jeff Kluttz, as
ReturningKing.com

Cover Art Images © [2011] Jupiterimages Corporation

Unless otherwise noted, scripture quotations are from The Holy Bible, English Standard Version® (ESV®), copyright © 2001 by Crossway, a publishing ministry of Good News Publishers. Used by permission. All rights reserved."

Scripture quotations marked "KJV" are taken from the Holy Bible, King James Version, Cambridge, 1769.

Scripture quotations marked (NIV) are taken from the Holy Bible, New International Version®, NIV®. Copyright © 1973, 1978, 1984, 2011 by Biblica, Inc.™ Used by permission of Zondervan. All rights reserved worldwide.

Scriptures taken from the NEW AMERICAN STANDARD BIBLE®, Copyright © 1960,1962,1963,1968,1971,1972,1973,1975,1977,1995 by The Lockman Foundation. Used by permission."

Contents

Introduction 1
Chapter 1 - The Nature of Apostasy 7
Chapter 2 - Our Biblical Mandate 15
Chapter 3 - How We Got Here 23
Chapter 4 - Introduction to The Word of Faith Movement 37
Chapter 5 - Revelation Knowledge 41
Chapter 6 - Faith: The Omnipotent Entity 55
Chapter 7 - Elevating Man to Godhood 69
Chapter 8 - The Demotion of God 79
Chapter 9 - Atonement Heresy: Kenoticism 93
Chapter 10 - Atonement Heresy: Jesus in Hell 107
Chapter 11 – Atonement Heresy: Jesus' Salvation 127
Chapter 12 - Healing in the Atonement 147
Chapter 13 – Guaranteed Wealth 167
Chapter 14 - The Biblical Response 195
Conclusion 205
Scripture Reference 223

> Jude 1:4 (KJV)
> ⁴ For there are certain men crept in unawares, who were before of old ordained to this condemnation, ungodly men, turning the grace of our God into lasciviousness, and denying the only Lord God, and our Lord Jesus Christ.

Introduction

A cancer is spreading at an alarming rate in the modern church. It expresses a heretical doctrine which exchanges the glory of the gospel of Christ for temporal gains that were once known as the very temptations of man. Heresy has become mainstream in a growing population of Christendom. Sadly, much of the church today is too biblically illiterate to notice. The concept of orthodoxy has been given over to a competitive attitude by which doctrine is relegated to a local flavor.

While heresy has always existed in the church, never has there been a time when "exotic and unfamiliar" were considered the creative virtues of preaching that they are today. The past few hundred years have been celebrated as times when enigmatic and incomprehensible creeds have been taken to task by a doctrinally savvy congregation and errors reproved by the biblical preaching of proven men of God. The tables seem to have turned entirely. In today's religious circles it is old-school holdouts with the audacity to cling to the scriptures that are in the minority. It is a truly remnant church which continues to preserve sound biblical fundamentals at the persistent ridicule of a new majority of doctrinal thrill-seekers.

Impostors of the faith scream dissent from thousands of books, television networks and millions of websites. Entire supposedly "Christian" publishing houses have abandoned their former biblical faith principles in favor of new proposals which, frankly, move more books off of store shelves. Christian bookstores, devoted more to their bottom line than the Lord's, have likewise lifted not one finger in any measurable way to dissuade this new trend. Numerous are the modern congregations which have jumped an entire generational cog; having an old-guard too tired or unwilling to fight for doctrinal purity and a new, younger work force that will only bother to show up if things are considered hip, novel, and decidedly not-too-biblical. Bereans are sparse; having been rapidly replaced by giddy, temperamental consumer-types who crave the latest "star" pastor's deposition over the eyewitness testimonies of the apostles. The recipe for the modern pulpiteer calls for less scriptural content and more bizarre showmanship, to the extent of being positively juvenile.

Evangelicalism is in sincere trouble. Authentic Christians are relegated to a tireless search to find a church that preaches the Bible at all, as today's pulpits more commonly stream self-help infomercials which refuse to mention, let alone offer remedy for man's greatest issue: *sin* and man's need for redemption. Churches have redefined ministry and missions in the image of public service fraternities. The gospel being proclaimed in so many supposedly "thriving" congregations is shallow enough to disappoint a Unitarian. Reminiscent are Jesus' words to the church in Sardis, "You have the reputation of being alive, but you are dead."[1]

Fueling these trends is a growing number of pastors who have committed themselves to unadulterated apostasy on the grounds that it produces the desired results. This new breed of pseudo-theologian teaches, through contrived and corrupt exegetical processes, things which in some cases *completely reverse* the truths of scripture. Man is instructed not on his depravity and need for salvation, but on his alleged posture of value before God's grateful eye. Christ is presented not as the crucified lamb but the exemplary enabler of human potential. Scripture is not promoted as the inspired testimony of God by which men are convicted, redeemed and trained for His eternal service, but the means by which they can learn the secrets of acquiring their best life now.

While such a dire state of the church is heart breaking to those who love her, it is not something which has taken the student of God's word by surprise. This emerging apostasy has been articulately forewarned in scripture; a word of caution to each generation that the roots of their faith will be challenged from within at a future juncture.

> *2 Timothy 4:3-4 (ESV)*
> [3] *For the time is coming when people will not endure sound teaching, but having itching ears they will accumulate for themselves teachers to suit their own passions,* [4] *and will turn away from listening to the truth and wander off into myths.*

Surely such times are now at hand. Paul could not have more articulately portrayed the state of the modern church. The tested and proven methodology of starting

---

[1] Revelation 3:1

new churches today is to send a group of surveyors into a neighborhood to determine the type of church that neighborhood would want to support. We are, in effect, asking *the lost* to dictate the function and direction of the church! We may as well be determining which fast food franchise to inject into a business center.

With the platform for church growth being the edification of everything people want to hear, the typical modern church has become little more than another consumer-oriented business. To the upwardly mobile, churches promise a leadership role in the renovation of culture. They are assured to be doing the work of Christ simply because they engage themselves in the types of things that Jesus did. To the poor and lowly is a promise of redemption; not from sin, but from the poverty which has stricken them due to their lack of "proper application" of God's Word. To the ill is the promise of God's full earthly reversal of their sicknesses, if only they will learn how to properly ask him. The church has become utterly user-friendly, offering carefully researched theological *products* which are in demand by the intended congregational target.

Numerous are the magical prayer books which give the correct formulas for invoking God's response to one's request, as if He were a cosmic genie who must only be suitably addressed for his magic to work. At the end of this process, man has taken the role of deity, dictating his will to an obedient subordinate; and God himself is presumed to be that humble servant. With cleverly orchestrated theological arguments which attempt to make this approach seem biblical, these false teachers have relegated man to a place of power, success and great personal glory, while almighty God becomes nothing more than a grand enabler of man's creative capacity.

Shortly, even Shirley McClain will be pleased to join one of our mainstream mega-church congregations.

In the charismatic world, the "Word of Faith" movement represents the largest organized purveyor of these types of consumer-oriented doctrines. This work will focus specific attention to this movement in the hopes of illuminating the truths of scripture as a warning to the millions who are being systematically indoctrinated by this group. Through religious television networks and an increasing number of local congregations buying into the sheer hype, the Word of Faith movement has generated non-stop sensationalistic and unverifiable claims that challenge everything formerly identified as orthodox faith. This work is not an attempt to engage heresy in debate, but to reveal it to individual readers for what it is. The true church must understand the nature of what she will battle in the coming days and years. These groups are steadily permeating the wheat field with tares while a lost and dying world is being cross-evangelized by false apostles utterly incapable of presenting the true gospel; for they do not know it themselves.

The end result of this counterfeit ministry will be an ever increasing wake of souls who are either happily deceived and relegated to an eternity of death, or are so damaged from their failed foray into "religion" that they write off Christ entirely as a charlatan who must be of the same essence as his phony ministers. Too often the deceived think they have experienced the fullness of Christ's grace and find it lacking. Sadly, many walk away from anything with the name of Christ attached to it from that point forward.

To that end, the responsibility of identifying and preaching against false doctrines is of major importance to those who live to affirm and defend the teachings of scripture. While scripture clearly indicates that an apostasy waits the latter days, it nevertheless demands the faithful of Christ to contend earnestly for the truth which transcends all times and cultures.

As Jude warns,

> ***Jude 1:3-4 (ESV)***
> *³ Beloved, although I was very eager to write to you about our common salvation, I found it necessary to write appealing to you to contend for the faith that was once for all delivered to the saints. ⁴ For certain people have crept in unnoticed who long ago were designated for this condemnation, ungodly people, who pervert the grace of our God into sensuality and deny our only Master and Lord, Jesus Christ.*

Chapter 1 - The Nature of Apostasy

Considering that "apostasy" is the very namesake of this work it is essential that a technical understanding of the term be presented. The term is misused at times to refer to common heresy and/or malpractice of the faith. While such *may be* apostasy, it is not necessarily so defined. Or, to put it another way, all apostasy is heresy, but not all heresy is apostasy.

The *term* and the *idea* of apostasy are noted numerous times in scripture; in both the Old and New Testaments. In most of the New Testament usages, apostasy is defined as a "falling" or a "falling away." Several times, apostasy is called out specifically by name with the use of the Greek term *apostasia,* a term which means "to defect" or "to revolt" from one's former orthodox position. *Apostasia* has as its root the preposition *apo,* which means "apart from" or "away from" and is combined with *stasis* ("to stand") to formulate an articulate definition of, "one who departs from an established position to pursue another."

Apostasia is also related to the term, *aphistemi,* meaning "to lead away" or "to depart from." Another related term is *apostasion,* which is translated "divorcement" or "divorce" in both the New Testament and the Septuagint.[2] Thus, the idea of "apostasy" clearly represents a departure

---

[2] Matthew 5:31, Matthew 19:7, Mark 10:4, Septuagint: Deuteronomy 24:3, Isaiah 50:1, Jeremiah 3:8

from that which is the subject of the term. Apostasy is a falling away or leading away from a formerly held position.

When used in reference to matters of the faith the term refers, of course, to having "fallen away" from the truth, or from orthodoxy. While many understand apostasy as nothing more than heresy, there is more fundamental meaning in the term than a simple correlation to being "wrong" about the truth. To be apostate is to have *fallen* away from the truth – not simply to "be" away from the truth.

Thus, while all apostasy is heresy, not all heresy is apostasy, for not every heretic has *chosen to abandon* a truth once rightly known and upheld. Some heretics have simply never known the truth at all. Pagans and proponents of false religious systems are heretics by definition, but are not apostates. Their condemnation, according to the scriptures, is still imminent but their heresy is due to having been taught wrongly or perhaps even from having heard and staunchly rejected the truth. However, to be apostate is to *have had the truth in possession* and to have *fallen away from* it. Unlike a common heretic – who may or may not know better – an apostate is one who formerly possessed a right understanding of the very truth which they have since rejected. To be apostate is to literally have heard, known, understood and claimed the truths of the faith and to have at a later time intentionally discarded them in favor of something else entirely.

Charles Ryrie notes that, *"apostasy is a departure from truth previously accepted and it involves the breaking of a professed relationship with God."*[3] Thus, it must be understood that an apostate is a very special kind of heretic: he is one who knows better!

It is precisely this understanding of the term noted by Paul when he writes,

> **2 Thessalonians 2:1-3 (ESV)**
> *[1] Now concerning the coming of our Lord Jesus Christ and our being gathered together to him, we ask you, brothers, [2] not to be quickly shaken in mind or alarmed, either by a spirit or a spoken word, or a letter seeming to be from us, to the effect that the day of the Lord has come. [3] Let no one deceive you in any way. For that day will not come, unless the rebellion comes first, and the man of lawlessness is revealed, the son of destruction....*

In this text Paul clearly speaks of a latter day reality, noting that "the day of the Lord" will not occur until an *apostasia* occurs. In this case, Paul speaks not of some undisclosed future apostate movement, but of a specific, foreknown one. While the KJV translates "a falling away" for this rendering, the Greek text notes *ho apostasia,* or *"the* apostasy." *Ho* is a definite article, rightly translated by the English term "the," rather than "a" or "an." As opposed to "an" apostasy, which is an indefinite article, *the* apostasy speaks with distinction concerning a peculiar apostasy; a *specific* apostasy. The apostasy in question is not one of many possible fall-out movements, but *the* apostasy of some previous reference which we must assume the recipients in Thessalonica would understand. It seems clear that Paul had taught them concerning the day of the Lord as he noted in 1 Thessalonians 5:2 that, *"you yourselves are fully aware*

---

[3] Charles C. Ryrie, "**Apostasy** in the Church," *Bibliotheca Sacra* 121 (January 1964): 46.

that the day of the Lord will come like a thief in the night." Perhaps he had taught them formerly of this apostasy that would precipitate the coming of Christ. He certainly taught the principle to Timothy.

In his first letter to Timothy Paul particularly noted a latter day apostasy. He declares specifically,

> **1 Timothy 4:1 (ESV)**
> [1] Now the Spirit expressly says that in later times some will depart from the faith by devoting themselves to deceitful spirits and teachings of demons.

Clearly an issue for "latter times," just as his counsel to the Thessalonians noted a "day of the Lord" warning, Paul once again refers to a coming apostate movement that will precede the day of the Lord. In this text he uses the root form (*aphistemi*) of the term, clearly detailing an event consistent with our understanding of apostasy. He notes that these latter-day people *"will depart from the faith."* One surely cannot "depart from" something of which one has never been near. Clearly this departure is that of people who are in the very least educated in matters of the faith. Clearly they know better. Plainly they are leaving the teachings they have known for something else. Incidentally, Paul does not note a mere side-stepping to a "light" version of the truth, but a turning aside entirely by *"devoting themselves to deceitful spirits and teachings of demons!"* The demonic influence of the latter day apostasy is also a recurring theme in scripture and should not be overlooked. But it is clear that Paul speaks to Timothy concerning the same apostate scenario of which he speaks to the Thessalonians. In his second letter he further notes,

> **2 Timothy 4:3-4 (ESV)**
> [3] ... the time is coming when people will not endure sound teaching, but having itching ears they will

> *accumulate for themselves teachers to suit their own passions,* [4] *and will turn away from listening to the truth and wander off into myths.*

In this text another similar term, *apostrepho,* is used in the very same manner and circumstance. This term, having the same meaning- "to turn aside" or "pervert"- is once again applied to those who formerly had access and tutelage in the matters of truth. They *"turn away from listening to the truth."* They *"wander off into myths."* While it is bad enough to scorn sound teaching out of ignorance or obstinacy, these men will have turned deliberately away from their diet of truthful indoctrination in order to pursue myths which better suit their sinful passions.

It is also possible that Paul notes *the* apostasy to the Thessalonians because of its first mention by none other than Christ himself as he warned the disciples in his Olivet Discourse,

> **Matthew 24:10-11 (ESV)**
> [10] *And then many will fall away and betray one another and hate one another.* [11] *And many false prophets will arise and lead many astray.*

Likewise, speaking of the season of the end, prior to the day of the Lord, Christ had formerly noted a falling away would occur. Christ's term is neither *apostasia, aphistemi* nor *apostrepho.* Rather, he uses *skandalizo,* the root from which our term "scandalize" originates. This term refers to one being entrapped, tripped up, or enticed into sin. Once again, the clear meaning of that which is an apostasy is being depicted. One cannot be tripped up if one were not first walking rightly. One cannot be guilty of scandal if he were not first understood to live in light of an appropriate standard.

These are strong examples of an ongoing principle throughout both the Old and New Testaments which depict a latter day apostasy to occur among people who claim to follow the Lord. Obviously the people of the Lord are none other than the professed church of the Lord Christ. It is from among the church that such scandal will arise and men will betray one another by falling away from the truth and into error.

As this work continues, a very specific type of heretic will be displayed. This work is not concerned with the heresies of false religions, although they certainly are to be preached against and avoided. This work will not focus on the weird and unusual heresies of those who were wrongly indoctrinated and have continued the legacy handed to them. This work will be focused on the worst heretic of all: the apostate.

The men who will be named by name and called out by doctrine in this work are men who have established an identity within the very church age which Christ is warning. These men have served as pastors and teachers. Many have seminary training and even Ph.D. credentials. They are not ignorant or ill-equipped men who sauntered unwittingly into sin. They are not merely of a false religious heritage which they have never challenged. They are those who have known and professed the truth and become willfully disobedient to it because it does not serve their appetites. Sadly, it is the church, in every case, who has given them a platform from which to spew their renegade doctrines. It is the church that has provided them audience and sanctuary. Likewise, in almost every circumstance, these men at some earlier point in their lives taught at least *fairly* accurate doctrine. Many never taught exceptional doctrine, mind you, but they at least taught that which could be considered within the boundaries of normative biblical faith. They understood and even preached the right message of the gospel. They preached and at least *seemed* to accept the divinity of Christ. They did not formerly espouse silly stories of self-verified encounters with Christ nor accuse the impoverished of being guilty of sin. They did in fact come from a full range of arguable traditions, yet would not formally have been considered heretical by the messages they taught during their earlier work. Nevertheless, one by one these impostors have revealed their true identities as their fruit has come into season.

Chapter 2 - Our Biblical Mandate

The proliferation of heresy in the church was such an alarm to Jude that he was inspired to change the entire subject matter of his epistle, noting:

> **Jude 1:3-4 (ESV)**
> [3] *Beloved, although I was very eager to write to you about our common salvation, I found it necessary to write appealing to you to contend for the faith that was once for all delivered to the saints.* [4] *For certain people have crept in unnoticed who long ago were designated for this condemnation, ungodly people, who pervert the grace of our God into sensuality and deny our only Master and Lord, Jesus Christ.*

This very admonition to contend for the true faith is one which must be addressed before engaging the study of specific apostate teachers. Invariably, there are some who will object to even the suggestion that popular Bible teachers be illuminated and held accountable for their records. I have lost fellowship with more than one person over my proclivity to proclaim heresy when I see it. I was scolded by one woman, as she left my teaching out of protest for her false television shepherd, "you should leave these men alone and just preach the Bible!" I was in fact preaching through the Sermon on the Mount! What better means to preach about wolves in sheep's clothing than to reveal a few examples?

But many do not share my zeal for defending the scriptures, especially when such becomes oriented toward their star personalities. Indeed, numerous false teachers themselves attempt to find asylum by quoting, "*touch not the Lord's anointed*" from Psalm 105:15. I assure you that anyone who has to hang their reputation on that abused line is *not* the Lord's anointed, nor are they called into account nearly often or loudly enough.

Still, there exists a fear among average believers of raising their voices against false prophets; partially, perhaps, because of their own lack of certainty as to what their role should be in such circumstances. Who wants to condemn people who teach about Jesus? Commonly, biblical ignorance fuels one's contentment for a lack of proper action. However scripture has much to say about the believer's responsibility in addressing and responding to those who corrupt God's word. Suffice it to say, "Teaching about Jesus" is not the same as declaring the gospel of Christ and rightly dividing the word of truth. Muslims, Mormons, Jehovah's Witnesses and witches "teach about Jesus." Politicians, historians and P.E. coaches "teach about Jesus." The issue is whether or not their teachings are *correct* according to the scriptures. If they are not, God's Word demands that we who are biblical must react against them, and that we are in fact *held accountable* for our failure to do so.

Even in the times before a canonized scriptural record was available, God held his people accountable for testing and vetting the prophetic vision of those who presumed to speak for God. Jeremiah emphatically called Israel to reject the teachings of false prophets, or risk sharing in their judgment.

> ***Jeremiah 14:14-16 (ESV)***
> [14] *And the LORD said to me: "The prophets are*

> *prophesying lies in my name. I did not send them, nor did I command them or speak to them. They are prophesying to you a lying vision, worthless divination, and the deceit of their own minds.* [15] *Therefore thus says the LORD concerning the prophets who prophesy in my name although I did not send them, and who say, 'Sword and famine shall not come upon this land': By sword and famine those prophets shall be consumed.* [16] *And the people to whom they prophesy shall be cast out in the streets of Jerusalem, victims of famine and sword, with none to bury them—them, their wives, their sons, and their daughters. For I will pour out their evil upon them.*

It is painfully obvious that God has no patience whatsoever for having his name profaned by liars. Nor is he tolerant of those who accommodate such work by listening and following their phony advice. Not only were the people told to reject the false teachers, but were themselves promised that God would "*pour out their evil upon them*" for allowing such teachings to be circulated! While many today cry for a bit of sentimental forbearance toward the heretics among us, the scripture in no way supports those who choose to "live and let live" concerning its own testimony. Quite contrarily, it emphatically demands that false teachers be tested and the substance of their doctrines be displayed as error by the true people of God.

Furthermore, false teachers are not only to be reprimanded, but disenfranchised from their positions because of such error. They are not to be allowed to present half-truths for the benefit of the more appealing half. Never is it observed in scripture that false teachers are to be heard for whatever good they may accidentally conjure up. At no time is there a "spit out the bones" policy reserved for those who speak out of step with God's word. Instead, false teachers are spoken of in terms which can only be related to God's enemies. They are called "delusional," "lying," "diviners," "polluters," "savage," "deceitful workmen," "servants of Satan," "conceited," and every other discriminating term imaginable.[4] Indeed, almost every New Testament author addresses false teachers or false teachings to some degree. Some do so numerous times and with great intensity. Devoid of political correctness doctrine, the scriptures adamantly portray these men as Satan's agents who will pay eternally for their crimes against the Lord. They are not called "misguided, but well-intentioned faith representatives," but those who, *"...claim to know God, but by their actions they deny him. They are detestable, disobedient and unfit for doing anything good."*[5]

Beyond merely acknowledging the existence of false shepherds, scripture demands clearly for believers to actively expose their error. As Paul instructs Timothy concerning his pastoral role, he unwaveringly asserts,

> ***1 Timothy 4:1-6 (ESV)***
> *[1] Now the Spirit expressly says that in later times some will depart from the faith by devoting themselves to deceitful spirits and teachings of demons, [2] through the insincerity of liars whose consciences are seared, [3] who forbid marriage and require abstinence from foods that God created to be received with thanksgiving by those who believe and know the truth. [4] For everything created by God is good, and nothing is to be rejected if it is received with thanksgiving, [5] for it is made holy by the word of God and prayer. [6] If you put these things before the brothers, you will be a good servant of*

---

[4] Jer. 14:14, Jer. 23:26, Jer. 29:8, Mat. 24:11, 2 Cor. 11:13-15, 1 Tim. 6:3-4

[5] Titus 1:16

> *Christ Jesus, being trained in the words of the faith and of the good doctrine that you have followed.*

Not only acknowledging the evil works of these teachers, Paul also exhorts Timothy to be involved in their illumination. He notes, "*If you put these things before the brothers, you will be a good servant of Christ Jesus.*" Inversely, one should surmise that to *fail* to point out the teachings of these hypocrites is tantamount to *not* being a good servant of Christ. Ironically, pastors today are commonly criticized for rightly pointing out the false teachings of the impostors of our faith when they should be commended, thanked and valued for the willingness to do that very biblical task.

Paul's commission concerning false teachers is to make a public spectacle of them, issue a public rebuke and institute verbal correction of their error. He clearly sees the work of such charlatans as a clear and present danger to the church,

> **Titus 1:10-14 (ESV)**
> [10] *For there are many who are insubordinate, empty talkers and deceivers, especially those of the circumcision party.* [11] *They must be silenced, since they are upsetting whole families by teaching for shameful gain what they ought not to teach.* [12] *One of the Cretans, a prophet of their own, said, "Cretans are always liars, evil beasts, lazy gluttons."* [13] *This testimony is true. Therefore rebuke them sharply, that they may be sound in the faith,* [14] *not devoting themselves to Jewish myths and the commands of people who turn away from the truth.*

Similarly, he notes to Timothy,

> **1 Timothy 1:3-4 (ESV)**
> [3] *As I urged you when I was going to Macedonia, remain at Ephesus so that you may charge certain persons not to teach any different doctrine,* [4] *nor to devote themselves to myths and endless genealogies,*

which promote speculations rather than the stewardship from God that is by faith.

The commission to *"charge"* these men *"not to teach any different doctrine, nor to devote themselves to myths"* is a nail in the coffin of the ideology that the church should be silent or empathetic of those who teach what is contrary to the scriptures. There is simply *no permissible reason* for one to preach false doctrine to the church. One popular pastor today takes great pains to note that he hasn't studied or investigated certain areas of the faith that he unwittingly defends. If that is the case, this man should cease to presume to be a pastor until he has readied himself for that task. He will not find asylum for his dereliction of duty from the Lord.

Lastly, it should be noted that rebukes against false teachers are to be utterly public and specific. While some biblical directives against false teachers are general in nature, such should not be interpreted as a sign that these con artists should be dealt with categorically, rather than specifically. In scripture are also numerous opportunities taken by God's leaders to call out false teachers *by name* in their local settings that the church may be properly warned. Thus, not only is it our duty to dispute and correct false doctrines when they are espoused, but it is our imperative to name names as unique and specific warning to the unwitting sheep who may be listening to these impostors.

Paul named names.

> *2 Timothy 2:16-18 (ESV)*
> [16] *... avoid irreverent babble, for it will lead people into more and more ungodliness,* [17] *and their talk will spread like gangrene. Among them are Hymenaeus and Philetus,* [18] *who have swerved from the truth, saying*

that the resurrection has already happened. They are upsetting the faith of some.

Luke named names.

> **Acts 13:6 (ESV)**
> [6] *When they had gone through the whole island as far as Paphos, they came upon a certain magician, a Jewish false prophet named Bar-Jesus.*

Jesus named names.

> **Revelation 2:20 (ESV)**
> [20] *But I have this against you, that you tolerate that woman Jezebel, who calls herself a prophetess and is teaching and seducing my servants to practice sexual immorality and to eat food sacrificed to idols.*

And I will name names in following their examples.

It should be equally warned, of course, that there are all manners of unnecessary insult within the legitimate body of Christ. Numerous are the books, websites and other public declarations calling for the ruination of solid Christian leaders over some disagreement concerning the minutiae of theological matters. Undoubtedly, Christ does not intend for the body to be divided over issues which are disputable in scripture. Romans 14 goes into great detail to note that the disputable areas of scripture are not to be the substance of quarrel or division. The local church is not called to raise arms against every other denomination which disagrees with its own in obscure matters of the faith. The body is fractured enough, frankly, without such additional ramblings of theological debate. Paul stated,

> **Romans 14:1 (ESV)**
> [1] *As for the one who is weak in faith, welcome him, but not to quarrel over opinions.*

The key to naming names and attacking error according to our biblical mandate is in properly centering such judgment on matters of faith that are biblically clear and essential; as opposed to those which are imprecise and arguable. While churches may disagree on the details of spiritual gifts or the proper ideology for church governance, such issues are not grounds for the types of public outcry and reprimand which are called for in regard to false teachers. In every case noted above, the false teachers in question are far beyond the boundaries of "disputable" theology. They are, in fact, utterly redefining the faith and changing the message of the gospel by their mishandling of God's Word. They are propagating the myths of their own minds. They are changing grace into a license for immorality. They are causing divisions for their own personal gain. And, they are so misrepresenting the gospel that it becomes no gospel at all. These people are under a motivation contrary to that of the Holy Spirit. They are not among those who struggle legitimately over the deep things of God, but those who for the cause of their particular purposes intentionally pervert God's word into their own image.

Chapter 3 - How We Got Here

The true gospel is - and always has been - by Christ, from Christ and for Christ. At any point this understanding is corrupted, apostasy is sure to follow. If salvation is not *by* Christ, then it is by some other means which will ultimately take Christ's place as the author and sustainer of salvation. The most obvious example of this is the Roman Catholic Church, which after corrupting its gospel to a sacramental and sacerdotal system of works, allowed such human acts to become more important than Christ's own work in the church's now-corrupted doctrine of salvation. If salvation is not *from* Christ, then it has another source as its guarantor which deserves our rightful worship. Most commonly in modern apostasy salvation is falsely reported to stem from one's own religious investments rather than God's grace. The common sentiment is that while perhaps Christ secured the means of salvation, the application of this provision is a uniquely human act. In that case, it is almighty man who receives the glory from the transaction. If salvation is not *for* Christ, then it becomes yet another in a long line of readily available *products* by which man's existence is enhanced. The gospel, in this circumstance, is not about God redeeming lost humanity to Himself. It is rather about man "finding God" and harvesting the fruition of that endeavor for his own use. This corruption of the gospel leads to an all too familiar man-centered understanding of atonement. That general misconception is that salvation "is all about me."

It takes very little self-interest for sinful man to defile the best of ideals. Once salvation becomes "all about me" then it is only a mild step until a television preacher can convince you that indeed Christ suffered, bled and died so that you could have all of the comforts in life that Christ never concerned himself with. An ego-centric gospel, when full blown, develops the local church into a self-help service center by which Christian products are circulated to meet the various personal wishes of its constituency. It is not at all uncommon today to hear the sentiment on tele-church that Jesus died for one's debts, disappointments and diseases – without a hint spoken of sin.

Several decades back this self-service approach to the faith generated a church growth venture which captured the true spirit of American capitalism and wielded it as biblical truth. This movement profoundly changed the direction of the modern congregation overall; primarily in America, but around the world as well. Robert Schuller was an early adopter of a church growth model which would blossom in following decades. Schuller's very business-like approach was to "give the people what they want." Supply-side religion was thus born into the greatest consumer culture the world has ever known. Men like Bill Hybels and Rick Warren helped to pioneer the most recent rendition of this crusade which systematically attempted to change the functional church growth model from gospel centered to growth centered. With a constant eye trained on a numerical growth-oriented valuation of the local church, these men and others like them methodically brainwashed an entire generation of pastors into a temporal success-driven church growth paradigm (where "success" equals "filled pews," "satisfied parishioners" and "strong offerings"). Gone were the days of shaking the dust off of one's feet where the gospel was rejected. Instead, men were called to reinvent the gospel until it produced the desired results.

As a young minister in the early 90s I attended a church growth conference in Houston, Texas with the entire staff of the church I served. I distinctly recall Rick Warren's testimony concerning the establishment of Saddleback Church, the shining monument to the success of and therefore the presumed merit of Warren's growth model. He explained exactly *how* he was able to establish such a large and "successful" church. It was certainly different from how I had learned that church growth was supposed to happen. Warren's testimony was that he exhaustively conducted door to door surveys in their California neighborhoods, approaching local (lost) citizens and asking them "what type of church" they would want to attend. After compiling the results of his intensive surveying work, long story short, he built a church that matched the market demands of his neighborhood. Warren continued to explain to us that based on his statistical insights we ministers of the gospel should spend less time worrying about theology and understand that no one in our congregations cared what the underlying Greek terms were for any portion of biblical text. Rather than boring our people with such doctrinal tedium, he noted that we should focus our preaching on twenty minute "how to" sermons aimed at topics that were frankly, irrelevant to the legitimate gospel needs of our congregation. Our focus should be on holding their attention (while they died in their sins, perhaps) with subjects like "How to Have a Healthy Marriage" or "How to Raise Children to be Leaders." While I have no bona-fide position from which I can doubt Warren's motives, I have every reason to castigate this method of church growth. It is the proverbial promotion of inmates to prison guards to ask a lost and dying world how the church of Jesus Christ should function.

From these types of tactics a new modus operandi has been established as an essentially capitalistic approach to "doing church." This is certainly not the doing of Schuller, Warren or Hybels alone, but a collective venture of a new breed of entrepreneurial pastors. The new strategies reduce prospective gospel converts to *customers* and the church is becoming a vendor of market-tested self-help product. Some have argued vehemently over this paradigm shift, noting that such serves as a gateway to church attendance, after which the gospel can be presented in small groups unto a legitimate harvest. Rarely, however, does the average "customer" desire to hear about his sin, condemnation and future destruction by God's righteous display of wrath concerning it. In too many cases the truth is all but abandoned except in the properly surveyed areas. Any difficult, challenging or scary portions of scripture are ignored altogether; quickly being replaced by the warmer and fuzzier in-demand doctrinal fodder. The gospel of Christ has been slowly replaced by self-interested ear-scratching platitudes in large portions of the modern church.

Such program based, market driven methodologies have become a "church planting 101" prototype in the modern age: *to plant a church, get a youth group to go door to door collecting surveys, find out what the people want from their church, hire a top notch implementation team who can deliver it and a good speaker who can sell it every Sunday.* We have now literally established in America a market-driven church model to enhance our overtly market-driven culture. The clear message, gospel optional, is to decisively emulate Schuller's "give the people what they want" method. Of course, this "new" method, at root level, isn't new at all. It is a warmed over, internet savvy recasting of the oldest religious shell game on earth. A big score has always awaited the one who could draw disciples off of the church, as the apostles continually warned even in their day.

When vast areas of the visible church attempt a truly market-driven approach to growth, foreign issues necessarily emerge on the harvest field. Markets cannot help but to be competitive by nature. If the church's vision is to win market share, then every other local church becomes a competitor and enemy of the cause. A new anti-cooperative arena is thus born whereby the goals and visions of the organization have nothing to do with the gospel, the corporate body or the ministry of Christ, but the success and veneration of the congregational brand – to the exclusion and repudiation of all others.

Contrarily, the *biblical* local church works in concert with other congregations to share the gospel to a lost world. No legitimate church considers itself anything but an extension of the body of Christ in a local field. A victory for another God-honoring church is a victory for us all (although God-honoring churches are now rather rare and hard to find). But a church which operates as a growth-oriented local business will find itself in necessary competition with other congregations; drawing off the dross of their rival by having a better or more marketable commodity.

This nature of the market driven church is noted profoundly in scripture as a characteristic framework from which an apostate operates: they work for their own gain rather than that of Christ. Scripture is chock full of warnings concerning how the false teacher works for the advancement of his personal "church business." They use their resources solely for the sake of drawing members. Members give. Giving pays the false teacher. Business boils down to filling pews by whatever means necessary. Paul asserts a warning of precisely this mentality in the book of Acts, noting,

> **Acts 20:29-30 (ESV)**
> ²⁹ *I know that after my departure fierce wolves will come in among you, not sparing the flock; ³⁰ and from among your own selves will arise men speaking twisted things, to draw away the disciples after them.*

In this text Paul is giving his parting words to the Ephesian elders. Having left them to pursue further missionary work, he is concerned with their awareness that false teachers will intentionally divide the flock that they may *"draw away the disciples after them."* Each false teacher, with his own desire to grow his individual empire, is necessarily unconcerned with the spiritual condition of the church. Using the imagery of a wolf to a flock Paul clearly depicts a scenario by which the false teacher considers the church to be nothing more than a meal ticket. Wolves have no relationship with sheep. Sheep are merely daily sustenance; or, if played right, even a lifetime of it. Paul warns similarly to the church at Galatia that

> **Galatians 4:17 (ESV)**
> ¹⁷ *They make much of you, but for no good purpose. They want to shut you out, that you may make much of them.*

The portrait Paul warns of throughout this epistle concerns the false teachers' fawning over the congregation to win their good favor; but only insomuch as the impostors believe they will have that favor returned to their own gain. Philippians 1:15 likewise notes, *"some indeed preach Christ from envy and rivalry."* In that context Paul specifically notes in verse 17 these wolves are attempting to steal his sheep to their own appetites, *"thinking to afflict me in my imprisonment."*

Such is the nature of a market. Competition is brutal. The winner takes the customer and his wallet. The loser

Apostasy! | 29

goes elsewhere. Paul never fails to warn congregations of this truth. To the Romans he notes,

> **Romans 16:17-18 (ESV)**
> [17] *I appeal to you, brothers, to watch out for those who cause divisions and create obstacles contrary to the doctrine that you have been taught; avoid them.* [18] *For such persons do not serve our Lord Christ, but their own appetites, and by smooth talk and flattery they deceive the hearts of the naive.*

Once again is noted the means by which the false teachers build their customer base; they *"cause divisions and create obstacles contrary to the doctrine that you have been taught."* In so doing, I might add, they follow the model of their own father, who in the Garden of Eden also muddied the clarity and logic of God's plainly spoken word by asking, *"Did God actually say, 'You shall not eat of any tree in the garden?'"*[6] The end result is that *"by smooth talk and flattery they deceive the hearts of the naïve"* and Satan's plan is replicated; once again discrediting God's work for the sake of the gain of the wolf.

To Timothy, Paul unconditionally notes,

> **1 Timothy 6:3-5 (ESV)**
> [3] *If anyone teaches a different doctrine and does not agree with the sound words of our Lord Jesus Christ and the teaching that accords with godliness,* [4] *he is puffed up with conceit and understands nothing. He has an unhealthy craving for controversy and for quarrels about words, which produce envy, dissension, slander, evil suspicions,* [5] *and constant friction among people who are depraved in mind and deprived of the truth, imagining that godliness is a means of gain.*

---

[6] Genesis 3:1

Again, the false teacher *"has an unhealthy craving for controversy."* Again he *"quarrels about words, which produce envy, dissension, slander,"* and every other divisive sentiment. The true motive of the wolf is exposed repetitively in scripture: he is *"imagining that godliness is a means of gain."* Paul continues his warning with the famous note that *"the love of money is a root of all kinds of evils. It is through this craving that some have wandered away from the faith and pierced themselves with many pangs."*[7]

To Titus Paul also warns that men teach false doctrines and divide the church for their own financial gain.

> ***Titus 1:11 (ESV)***
> *[11] They must be silenced, since they are upsetting whole families by teaching for shameful gain what they ought not to teach.*

He warns the Corinthian church concerning the proper method of local ministry:

> ***2 Corinthians 2:17 (ESV)***
> *[17] For we are not, like so many, peddlers of God's word, but as men of sincerity, as commissioned by God, in the sight of God we speak in Christ.*

The term "peddlers" in the ESV is *kapeleuo,* which means "to retail" in a dishonest method. The root of *kapeleuo* is *kapelos,* which refers to a huckster or a charlatan. Paul's clear intention is to distance his character in ministry from those who treat the scriptures as snake oil salesmen; with a lack of faith in their own testimony who press on for the sake of the sale.

> ***2 Peter 2:17-19 (ESV)***
> *[17] These are waterless springs and mists driven by a*

---

[7] 1 Timothy 6:10

> storm. For them the gloom of utter darkness has been reserved. ¹⁸ For, speaking loud boasts of folly, they entice by sensual passions of the flesh those who are barely escaping from those who live in error. ¹⁹ They promise them freedom, but they themselves are slaves of corruption. For whatever overcomes a person, to that he is enslaved.

Never in the scriptures are the motives of false teachers questioned. Always they are known: False teachers work for their own appetites and their own gain. Many today attempt to excuse apostates as having good intentions but bad training. Yet God's Word leaves no excuse to those who reject the training provided *in scripture itself*. They are called into account, condemned and proclaimed as enemies of Christ in every instance.

Clearly then, human traditions and cultural patterns are a suitable environment for false doctrines to be marketed by the opportunistic heretic. Such is the affirmation of scripture as Paul notes,

> ***Colossians 2:8 (ESV)***
> ⁸ See to it that no one takes you captive by philosophy and empty deceit, according to human tradition, according to the elemental spirits of the world, and not according to Christ.

Today's pop-savvy false shepherds are experts at extracting marketable doctrinal material from culture. Such is the very nature of the market driven church as it invests much time, energy and money in the discovery of neighborhood sentiment. Yet the scriptures declare with precision that there also exists a much more sinister power at work in the doctrines of false shepherds.

As I began biblical research on this subject I was actually surprised at the frequent connections between false teachers and demonology, divination and spiritism. The Bible is clear that heretical teachers are motivated by his lusts for money, power and fame, but they are also frequently condemned in scripture of a far worse offense, as demonic influence is tied repetitively throughout both Testaments with regard to the foundation of the message of false prophets.

It actually makes perfect sense that false teachers would be used particularly by Satan. Apostates, being unregenerate, are unknown by the Holy Spirit. They are victim to the wiles of our enemy without concern or knowledge. They are objects of God's wrath, lost in their sins, and subject to any and all deception of the demonic forces at large. Jesus noted the very same of the apostates of his day proclaiming,

> ***John 8:44 (ESV)***
> *⁴⁴ You are of your father the devil, and your will is to do your father's desires. He was a murderer from the beginning, and has nothing to do with the truth, because there is no truth in him. When he lies, he speaks out of his own character, for he is a liar and the father of lies.*

Thus, the apostate is not merely a misguided soul doing his best to shine a dim light on subjects he cannot possibly understand for his personal benefit. He is also the very agent of Satan, working for the purposes of he who has "no truth in him."

God, through Jeremiah, testified that

> ***Jeremiah 14:14 (ESV)***
> *¹⁴ ... "The prophets are prophesying lies in my name. I did not send them, nor did I command them or speak to them. They are prophesying to you a lying vision, worthless divination, and the deceit of their own minds.*

God's affirmation is that the false prophets of Jeremiah's day *spoke actual prophecies;* but lying ones. The term translated "vision" in this text is Hebrew *hazon*, which refers to both tangible and prophetic vision. This term is used of God's true prophets as freely as it is used of the false prophet in this text. The message of Jeremiah 14:14 is not that the vision is false – in the sense of it not being a true vision – but that it is false in the sense of it being a lie. The prophets of whom Jeremiah speaks are likely seeing actual visions- but they are not visions from God. They are presenting rather *"a lying vision, worthless divination, and the deceit of their own minds."* Once again, their visions may very well be real, but are the result of divination. They are Satanic in nature. Thus, their minds are deceived and they present the teachings of Satan as if they were the teachings of God.

This phenomenon is certainly not unique to Jeremiah's period. The New Testament is scattered with references to the very same types of scenarios. As noted earlier in Paul's warning to Timothy,

> *1 Timothy 4:1 (ESV)*
> [1] *Now the Spirit expressly says that in later times some will depart from the faith by devoting themselves to deceitful spirits and teachings of demons....*

This text, once again, speaks specifically of the apostate. *"Depart from the faith"* is the Greek term *aphistemi,* one of the terms rightly translated "apostasy" or "apostatize." Paul states, with the affirmation of the Holy Spirit, that a latter day apostasy will occur that is accurately represented as those who depart the faith *"by devoting themselves to deceitful spirits and the teachings of demons."* It is very hard to miss the clear warning given in the text. Apostasy is not a simple matter of differences of opinion or a repackaging of the truth in a trendier container. Apostasy – in this case specifically - is a departure from the truth which leads the apostate directly into the arms of demonic deception. While apostates have their own appetite as their goal they have demonic intervention as their doctrinal source. They are presenting *"the teachings of demons"* which came to them as the result of having been devoted to deceitful spirits.

Paul speaks separately to the Corinthian church about men who preach "a different gospel."[8] He notes that,

> ***2 Corinthians 11:13-15 (ESV)***
> [13] ... *such men are false apostles, deceitful workmen, disguising themselves as apostles of Christ.* [14] *And no wonder, for even Satan disguises himself as an angel of light.* [15] *So it is no surprise if his servants, also, disguise themselves as servants of righteousness. Their end will correspond to their deeds.*

Making no attempt to soften his blow, Paul not only calls them deceitful workmen, but *intentionally so.* These deceitful workmen are *disguising themselves* as apostles of Christ. One does not disguise himself unwillingly or unknowingly; but calculatedly and intentionally so. These men, noted to be *servants of Satan,* dress themselves up to appear as an apostle of Christ in the very manner that Satan disguises himself as an angel of light. Once again, the false apostle is not heralded as "a dissenting opinion which should be considered," but a *"deceitful workman"* whose *"end will correspond to (his) deeds."*

Debate continues to be bantered about in today's media-rich culture as to the proper response toward one who teaches heretical doctrines. Some will always attempt to defend the validity of an opposing view as an exercise of some transcendent fairness doctrine. Others will disagree while defending the false shepherd's right to be wrong. Some will confuse their domestic freedoms with theological license and express that everyone has "their

---

[8] 2 Corinthians 11:4

own version" of the truth to enjoy. But, for the biblical student, the decision to hold a teacher accountable is a simple one. The scriptures are uncompromising and articulate in their call for the condemnation of teachers who corrupt, defile and confuse good doctrine.

They are demonic.

They are of the enemy of Christ.

They are not to be overlooked or tolerated.

They are to be exposed, reprimanded and held in contempt for failure to repent. The apostles demonstrate no hesitation at all at doing precisely that. To that end, such open reprimand will be the approach of this work. May the false shepherds and those who follow them repent, turn to Christ and be redeemed of their sin.

Chapter 4 - Introduction to the Word of Faith Movement

With a consumer-oriented church growth model in hand, the modern proponents of what has been labeled the "Word of Faith" or "Word Faith" movement jumped head first into the brilliant marketing of doctrines that would please their clientele. The patrons they sought to woo were those of charismatic persuasion, particularly those who were prone to watch and contribute to Christian television ministries.

Let me be quick to establish that this work is not aimed at charismatic believers as a whole; but the particular group labeled "Word of Faith" (WoF). There are many charismatic believers that, while we may disagree on certain doctrinal issues, are right-thinking and have a biblical doctrinal view that falls within the arguable latitude of normative Christian faith standards. Much of the traditional charismatic movement, even within their disagreement with non-charismatics on issues such as the nature of spiritual gifts, has been faithful to an orthodox core of essential doctrines. A traditional and historic charismatic school of thought accepts and defends, for example, the substitutionary atonement of Christ. They understand that Christ is the Son of God, and that he was fully God throughout his earthly life. They know that salvation is by grace, through faith, and not something to be obtained by works. They understand that the scriptures are our standard of faith and are not to be bartered against by a supposed vision, dream or sensationalistic work which compromises clear biblical teaching.

Chapter 4 - Introduction to the Word of Faith Movement

The typical charismatic does, however, have an inbuilt desire to see the supernatural at work which has made them a favored audience for the WoF wolves. WoF teachers have strategized their system of doctrine – which is *hugely opposed* to traditional Pentecostal doctrines – to build upon that desire. In short, they have developed a "product" of false doctrine, complete with sensationalistic claims of supernatural signs and wonders that are fitting for the audience they have chosen to infiltrate. And infiltrate, they have.

It seems that the vast majority of new charismatic church growth and significant portions of pre-existing charismatic congregations are now embracing at least some elements of WoF doctrine. While not all have fully subscribed to the tenets of the WoF doctrines which will be examined in this work, one is hard pressed to find a modern charismatic church that has not succumbed to at least part of the WoF doctrinal agenda.

The Word of Faith movement is named for its assertion that spoken words are the containers which hold, harness and release a "force" of quasi-faith into the natural world. Such "spoken faith" is heralded as the means for a believer to presumably release or lay ahold of literally any and everything his heart desires. God's sovereignty and will are set aside, as the believer is given full access to this phantom tool by which they can command the universe by their words. This characteristic will be described more fully in Chapter 6, but is the core component of the movement, serving as the namesake and key doctrinal distinctive.

The modern rise of this movement is commonly credited to Kenneth E. Hagin, who borrowed, warmed over and popularized the heretical works of the very controversial 19th century pastor, E.W. Kenyon. It was however

Apostasy! | 39

Kenyon's eccentric teachings that have served as the base of theological principle by which the modern movement propagates. Hagin, affectionately called "Papa Hagin" by many in the movement, is believed to have had numerous personal encounters with God by which his understanding of the Word-Faith principles were strengthened. Yet, large portions of Hagin's writings can be found word-for-word in the earlier works of Kenyon, the true originator of the "name & claim" doctrine of the Word of Faith movement.

Kenyon's infamous quote, and the summary assertion of his belief system, was "What I confess, I possess." This statement establishes the principle behind the name "word of faith." Kenyon believed, as do his modern WoF followers, that the words one speaks in faith have mystical powers beyond even that of God himself, for the WoF teaches that even God uses this fraudulently defined "faith" as the basis for his own works.

Hagin developed the rough draft of what has become known as the basis of Word of Faith theology. It was then borrowed, embellished and redistributed by numerous other disingenuous teachers, many of whom have connections with Trinity Broadcasting Network, a substantial enabler and co-conspirator in the propagation of WoF doctrines.

The essence of such doctrine will be examined in light of scripture throughout the remainder of this work. Necessarily, however, if one's doctrine of faith is flawed, then one's understanding of the gospel is necessarily flawed; for it is by faith that one must be saved.[9] Doctrines are built upon and interdependent with other doctrines. To that end, the WoF is much more than a

---

[9] Ephesians 2:8, Romans 3:22, Romans 4:16

mere faulty set of definitions concerning the nature of biblical faith; it is an entire systematized theological order that has been gradually fabricated to support the logical conclusions of the word-faith heterodoxy. Because the doctrine of faith was redefined, soteriology (the doctrinal study of salvation) was necessarily likewise tweaked to support the earlier error. Like a school child, having told a small lie, might be instigated to invent bigger and bigger lies to support it, the doctrinal assertions of the WoF movement have systematically fallen to error in order to support their erroneous foundational principle of word-faith.

The extent of the saturation of WoF doctrines is truly impressive in modern charismatic circles. Certainly there are charismatic churches and organizations that consistently – and properly – teach *against* the WoF movement. However it has gained such global support overall that several predominantly charismatic television networks almost exclusively cater to WoF target audiences. Charismatic friends have told me that it is increasingly difficult to exist in their church circles without succumbing to WoF ideologies which increasingly are seen as a banner of superiority in the faith. Sadly, the teachings of the WoF movement are actually more likely indicators which point out those who have abandoned the faith altogether; having apostatized themselves to another gospel.

Chapter 5 - Revelation Knowledge

Before furrowing into the distinctions of doctrinal error regarding faith, a prerequisite doctrine necessary for the development of such notions must first be examined. While the scriptures are quite stealthily twisted and bent into contortions in order to support the WoF definition of faith, the glue that holds the doctrine together is the misuse of what is termed "revelation knowledge" by those in the movement.

"Revelation," as a theological term, refers essentially to the manner by which information is given to man by God. In classic and normative theological study, revelation has been understood to fall into two general categories; general and special.

General revelation refers to understanding of God which can be gleaned from the natural order of things. General revelation assumes no direct and specific injection of information to mankind *from God*, but rests on the natural order of the creation and what may visibly be determined without God having had to speak at all. As a temporal example, if a person visits a remote uncharted island and discovers statues of giant heads, he can then determine by general revelation that intelligent life had once occupied that island. Through general revelation, one cannot know who the giant heads belonged to, what their purpose was or what other truths about the heads may exist outside of what one's normal sensory input can reveal. One simply knows they are there, and they were put there by some intelligent being. Likewise, by general revelation one can know that God exists, but cannot know his law, his judgment for sin or his plan of redemption.

To the contrary, special revelation is the impartation of information to man which *cannot be understood* from the natural order of things and must thus be granted by a direct and specific injection of knowledge from God himself. In short, special revelation refers to those moments in history when God - through miraculous interruption of the natural order – spoke directly to man, as we believe by faith that He did to Moses, the prophets and the apostles.

Special revelation is the basis by which most doctrinal teachings in the scriptures were revealed to man. While a full study of special revelation is beyond the scope of this work, suffice it to say that historic Christian theology maintains that special, unique, divinely inspired revelation is the means by which God has made known the doctrines of scripture. Thus, special revelation is universally understood by those who love and trust the scriptures to be valid, impeccable and trustworthy in the biblical accounts.

"Revelation knowledge," in short, is a term used habitually by Word of Faith teachers to describe their supposed personal receipt of special revelation by God himself *outside of the scriptures*. They are, in effect, saying that God spoke to them new truths just as He did to Moses, the prophets and apostles. Just as the biblical authors received a conscious inbreathing of God's truth which were penned into the Bible itself, those declaring to have received revelation knowledge today are laying claim to the very same authority as the biblical writers: that God has spoken truth into their minds that could not have been revealed in any other way.

To that end the WoF understanding of the term, "revelation knowledge," by definition, is *God's Word* which has been passed from God to man in the modern age; after the close of the biblical canon. Furthermore, in the case of the modern WoF teacher, this purported "word from the Lord" can trump, erase, change or redefine what God has formerly spoken, confirmed and preserved in the very Bible they claim to believe and uphold.

At this point, a very fine line in the sand must be understood. I take no issue with the existence of special revelation. It is the means by which the scriptures came to pass. I take no issue with the validity of some aspect of special revelatory leadership by God being exercised today- in the sense that God communicates his will to man –through his Word – and confirms it through the gentle guidance of the Holy Spirit. The purpose of this work is not to repudiate God's ability to lead, guide and direct his subjects via divine means. The issue taken against the revelation knowledge claims of the WoF in this work are rather aimed at the fact that revelation knowledge is presumed to be as valid, binding and trustworthy as the very scriptures which were revealed by the same God at an earlier time. If God, who cannot lie, spoke truths to Moses, the prophets and the apostles thousands of years ago, he *cannot and will not change his Word today*; especially through the unsubstantiated testimony of a teacher who changes biblical theology into something altogether new.

The key distinguishing factor that defines God's legitimate communication to a disciple of Christ from what is dubbed "revelation knowledge" by the WoF teachers is the *confirmation of the scriptures*.

Any legitimate believer in Christ should take specific and aggressive dispute with the idea that God has authenticated a new message contrary to his written and established Word which was delivered to the apostles. And that is precisely what the revelation knowledge claims of the WoF teachers represent: God having spoken *to them alone* a new and counter-biblical message which is to be believed and upheld over the scriptures. The WoF understanding of "revelation knowledge," by definition, is a modern re-manifestation of *God's Word* which has been passed from God to the WoF teacher just as it was delivered to Moses.

Make no mistake that when a WoF proponent uses the term "revelation knowledge," they do not mean that God has confirmed in their spirits the teaching of scripture- such as when a sinner is convicted of sin or a man is called to the mission field from principles learned through biblical study and application. What they mean instead, is that, *"God has told me something that he hasn't told you or anyone else. It is not in the Bible, so you will just have to trust me about the new doctrines it establishes."*

It is this misapplication of revelation which is heralded persistently by WoF teachers as a means to establish verification of their doctrinal positions which do not align themselves with the written Word. It is precisely this extra-biblical revelatory pursuit which Jesus reprimanded the Sadducees for when he noted,

> **Matthew 22:29 (ESV)**
> [29] *But Jesus answered them, "You are wrong, because you know neither the Scriptures nor the power of God.*

In fact, Jesus regularly quoted the Old Testament scriptures to verify the truthfulness of his own teaching. He, the author of scripture in the flesh, felt it necessary to confirm himself with Moses and the prophets. Likewise, the apostles corroborated continually their teachings with the Old Testament, with Jesus's words and in full agreement with the other apostles.

Apostasy! | 45

Contrarily, the Word of Faith teacher simply says "thus saith the Lord" and the Christian community is expected to follow. Sadly, many do. This bogus injection of special revelation into the faith has become the weapon of choice by which a WoF teacher can literally invent doctrines without repercussion. It is sufficient in this movement to simply say, *"God told me,"* and provide a sensationalistic story to promote an authentic feel to the encounter. Such stories are told on Christian television with the regularity of seasonal sitcoms on other networks and are left utterly unchallenged and unverified by the faithful followers of the movement.

Paul warns sternly about such ignorance.

> ***Galatians 1:6-8 (ESV)***
> *⁶ I am astonished that you are so quickly deserting him who called you in the grace of Christ and are turning to a different gospel— ⁷ not that there is another one, but there are some who trouble you and want to distort the gospel of Christ. ⁸ But even if we or an angel from heaven should preach to you a gospel contrary to the one we preached to you, let him be accursed.*

Paul lucidly calls for the eternal condemnation of anyone, including an angel from Heaven, who changes the gospel of Christ. God does not change. Truth, which is defined by him, does not change. His word does not change. Rather, Paul asserts that any such change is a distortion of the true gospel. Isaiah likewise proclaims that,

> ***Isaiah 40:8 (ESV)***
> *⁸ The grass withers, the flower fades, but the word of our God will stand forever.*

Since the reformation, Protestants have underscored the Bible, and the Bible alone as the source of revelation (in contrast to Roman Catholicism which teaches the Bible plus history as the basis for revelation) for the essentials of the Christian faith. These essentials are understood to be eternally invariable in light of the unchanging nature of God's word which revealed them.

While God may certainly quicken someone to knowledge, such knowledge never usurps scripture, else it is considered utterly heretical. One cannot claim the scriptures *and* newly propagated revelation knowledge together, for the scriptures themselves prohibit any such variance from their own truths. The scripture – being the source of our faith – cannot be trumped by a "new" source of faith without itself becoming an object of scorn as a failed and invalid message! Paul noted contrarily that,

> *2 Timothy 3:16-17 (ESV)*
> *[16] All Scripture is breathed out by God and profitable for teaching, for reproof, for correction, and for training in righteousness, [17] that the man of God may be competent, equipped for every good work.*

Never in the post-canonical Christian faith has it been expected by any orthodox teacher or group that religious truth should come by the means of any other revelation than that of the scriptures. In fact, those historical groups which have added their own extra-biblical teachings and books are labeled "cults" and are excluded from inclusion in fellowship with the true church.

The inspiration of scripture is a fundamental element of orthodox Christianity. To change the gospel doctrine- by any means- according to Paul, is to be eternally condemned.

Yet, WoF teachers must depend on a substantial repertoire of "revelation knowledge" to hypothetically substantiate their doctrines. Any logical mind should find it decidedly clear that one can hardly substantiate one's own testimony *with one's own testimony!* Even while the premise is clearly erroneous, it is an understandable approach for them to take from the standpoint that the Bible does *not contain* their doctrines. As such, they cannot provide a legitimate validation of their claims, and must resort to a fabled extra-biblical source such as self-supported revelation knowledge. In fact, the *only* way to claim to follow the Bible and teach unbiblical doctrines is to assert something else as authoritative *beyond* the Bible itself. That something, in WoF teaching, is the unverifiable realm of revelation knowledge.

This is how the movement began with Hagin. As the commonly proclaimed "papa" of the movement, it was by direct revelation from Jesus in a vision that he purportedly received his teachings on prosperity. He notes,

> "The Lord Himself taught me about prosperity. I never read about it in a book. I got it directly from heaven"[10]

Such is precisely the problem. Those who support this movement are ready to believe Hagin, Copeland, Hinn and hundreds of others over the testimony of scripture. Sadly, the propping up of heresy in this manner is an extremely common and accepted practice in the WoF world. While the scriptures say *"faith comes by hearing, and hearing through the word of Christ,"*[11] WoF teacher, Joyce Meyer, refutes,

> "The Bible can't even find any way to explain this. Not really. That's why you've got to get it by revelation. There are no words to explain what I'm telling you. I've got to just trust God that He's putting it into your

---

[10] **Kenneth Hagin, Sr.** *How God Taught Me About Prosperity* (Tulsa: Faith Library, 1985)

[11] Romans 10:17

Chapter 5 - Revelation Knowledge

spirit like He put it into mine."[12]

Seriously? The Bible can't find a way to explain something and has to depend on Joyce Meyer to bring it to the world? Of all the things the Bible *does* explain which we can't begin to understand fully in this life, how brilliant Joyce Meyer must be to comprehend principles so profound that the Bible can't even express them! To wholly ponder the utter arrogance of such statements one must comprehend that the Bible was inspired by the Holy Spirit himself, according to 2 Timothy 3 (above). Is Meyer actually giving herself a promotion so lavish that she is capable of understanding what the Holy Spirit is *incapable* of expressing through the written Word?

Such statements comprise *Doctrinal Persuasion 101* in this movement. If you have a doctrine that you cannot find a biblical explanation for, you blame revelation knowledge for its existence in your head. Kenneth Copeland uses the same self-authenticating method to propagate his utterly blasphemous atonement theory, noting:

> "The Spirit of God spoke to me and He said, "Son, realize this. Now follow me in this and don't let your tradition trip you up." He said, "Think this way -- a twice-born man whipped Satan in his own domain." And I threw my Bible down... like that. I said, "What?" He said, "A born-again man defeated Satan, the firstborn of many brethren defeated him."[13]

---

[12] **Joyce Meyer**, *What Happened from the Cross to the Throne* (audio (now unavailable))

[13] **Kenneth Copeland**, *What Happened from the Cross to the Throne* (Fort Worth, TX: Kenneth Copeland Ministries, 1990)

Apostasy! | 49

The fictitious doctrine in this quote will be dealt with later, rest assured. But before even illuminating the apostate nature of the teaching, one can't help but notice Copeland's authentication methods are self-substantiating from the start: "The Spirit of God spoke to me and said..." How can one who believes in God's continuing and evolving revelation argue with that? Ken spoke directly to God and received a doctrine that *no one else in two thousand years* had been privy to. Opportunely, he notes that after he hears directly from God, "I threw my Bible down." This is the only part of his quote that I believe. He most certainly threw his Bible down at some point or another, for this assertion most certainly did not come from the scriptures.

Jesse Duplantis takes unverifiable knowledge to a whole new level, claiming to have been in the physical presence of God whereby he saw God and had conversations with him. Utterly denying the teachings of scripture in his video, *Close Encounters of the God Kind*, he quips that God "was taller than I thought He would be."[14]

Now, because of Duplantis' self-proclaimed "visit" to see God in the flesh, those who follow him are asked to reduce their Bibles to folklore. Immediately tossed aside are the ancient biblical notes that man cannot see God in his mortality and live.[15] Gone also are the terms of God's biblical descriptions – now trumped by Duplantis' round trip to Heaven - proclaiming God to have physical size and stature while the scripture clearly dictates that "*God*

---

[14] **Jesse Duplantis**, *Close Encounters of the God Kind* (Jesse Duplantis Ministries) Internet Availability Only

[15] Genesis 32:30, 33:20,

is spirit, and those who worship him must worship in spirit and truth."[16]

Such fantasy is immensely rampant in this movement. Television shows, public events, books and spectacles of all varieties note pompous testimonies of special revelation which thwarts the clear teachings of scripture. To that end, students are expected to trust the unverifiable revelation knowledge of the teachers, even though this knowledge *specifically repudiates* scripture's own testimony.

Finally, concerning the revelation knowledge fiasco being propagated in the WoF movement, it should be noted that not a shred of verification ever follows such ridiculous claims. Frankly, if WoF teachers would be content to stay general in their revelation knowledge shell game, they may get something right once in a while and the job of exposing them would be more difficult. Haughtily, they seem to believe their own rhetoric, yet history has proven their utterances to be inaccurate time and again.

While it is impossible to empirically investigate Copeland's conversations with the Lord or Duplantis' visit to Heaven, these teachers are cooperative to shower ridiculous "visions" on their adoring fan base at regular intervals which *are* able to be verified. They are almost always verified, in fact, as false.

These men make daily forays into the world of revelation knowledge; with supposed prophetic utterances that have become too numerous to count. Benny Hinn, live on a TBN broadcast with Steve Brock, had the arrogance to say that Ruth Heflin had

---

[16] John 4:24

Apostasy! | 51

Benny: "just sent me a word through my wife and said, the Lord spoke to her audibly and said that He is going to appear physically in one of our crusades in the next few months."

Steve Brock: "My God! I'm ready for that!"

Benny:" Yeah. She -- I'm telling you! -- she said, the Lord spoke to her audibly and said 'Tell Benny I'm going to appear physically on the platform in his meeting.'"[17]

As of the writing of this work, eleven years have passed and Hinn's prophecy has not come to pass. Is anyone seriously surprised? His purported revelation from God was clearly a hoax, or at best an extremely blatant mistake, yet he offered no apology, recant, repentance nor offering of explanation. Such happens so regularly that he can't afford to get into the detraction game at all.

Hinn prophesied in the 90's that before the year 2000 God would destroy America's homosexual community, the death of Fidel Castro, America would elect its first female president and that the east coast would be devastated by earthquakes.[18] One needs only to do a cursory check of history to find these claims to be nowhere near the truth. Yet, once again, Hinn continues walking on water in the eyes of his fans that seem not to notice the emperor's $10,000 suit is missing.

Kim Clement, a self-proclaimed prophet of God, is another example of revelation knowledge run amuck in this movement. He bragged audaciously on his own website in 2003 concerning his alleged prophetic vision.

---

[17] TBN televised broadcast, March 29, 2000, "This is Your Day"

[18] http://en.wikipedia.org/wiki/Benny_hinn

Chapter 5 - Revelation Knowledge

He proclaimed sternly that America would be entering war shortly (as if anyone in 2001 were unaware of that very likely chain of events) and fantastically, that not one American life would be lost in the war! He declares,

> On April 1st 2001, I said "America prepare yourself, you will go to war". Subsequently, the Spirit began to share some of the details about the possible length of the battle and the outcome. I spoke about certain attacks planned against the soldiers and the fact that God would protect them so that not one of them would be inflicted. I believe with all of my heart that America is in the perfect will of God. A tyrant lives, and yet there are people in this nation shouting the odds about the instrument that God has chosen as his battle-axe -- the President of the United States of America.[19]

How foolish is a man to blame God for his own delusion. Not only did he essentially call God a liar for the loss of American lives which followed but he also foolishly noted that America was "in the perfect will of God?!?" Obviously, thousands of Americans died in the second Gulf War conflict. For all of those who believe in Clement's testimony, God is now left holding the bag for the loss of life and the failure to follow through on what He reportedly had said. It is furthermore clear that any prophet who thinks America is in "the perfect will of God" is nothing less than delusional.

Many more examples of falsified revelation knowledge will be given throughout the course of this work, chiefly because much of the WoF doctrine is based on one of two

---

[19] From http://www.kimclement.com/newsflashes/newsflashes.htm, March 19th 2003 (article has since been removed)

things: a maligning of the scriptures or the imposition of imaginary revelation knowledge (in those instances when scripture can't sufficiently be twisted.)

These short examples easily relate the fallacy of the WoF revelation knowledge claims. All such assertions make the presumption that God has spoken, through a modern day prophet, truths that could not otherwise been known. Numerous revelation claims of the movement directly rebut scripture. In either case, such contentions are simply erroneous, fictional and wrong. They do not even come adjacent to reality.

When God revealed himself through the prophets of the past, there are several things that He never did. First, He *never contradicted what He had formerly spoken.* Such truth is precisely what Jesus meant when he noted,

> **Luke 21:33 (ESV)**
> *33 Heaven and earth will pass away, but my words will not pass away.*

God doesn't wake up in a new world every day and attempt to determine the signs of the times like a false teacher does. He is sovereign; holding full comprehension of all knowledge, history and truth. He who has omniscience has no cause nor course to change His words in light of new information. James notes,

> **James 1:17 (ESV)**
> *17 Every good gift and every perfect gift is from above, coming down from the Father of lights with whom there is no variation or shadow due to change.*

Secondly, God is never wrong in what He says. Even if God were so inclined as to bring a new revelation to his latter day disciples, an absolute certain proof that God *has not spoken* such testimony should be self-evident when it is revealed to be untrue.

> **Psalm 18:30 (ESV)**
> ³⁰ This God—his way is perfect; the word of the LORD proves true; he is a shield for all those who take refuge in him.

Make no mistake; under these circumstances the very foundation from which these teachers assert their spiritual authority is broken. The TRUE words of scripture maintain that a prophet of God *does not err* in his teaching.

> **Deuteronomy 18:22 (ESV)**
> ²² when a prophet speaks in the name of the LORD, if the word does not come to pass or come true, that is a word that the LORD has not spoken; the prophet has spoken it presumptuously. You need not be afraid of him.

Sadly, great fear of such false apostles is precisely the tool used by the WoF teacher to keep his (or her) flock in line. I implore true believers to turn aside from those who tell lies in the name of the Truth. God *has not spoken* that prophecy which fails to come to pass.

Chapter 6 - Faith: The Omnipotent Entity

As introduced in chapter four, a completely inaccurate understanding of the nature of faith is an essential component of the WoF doctrinal malaise. The movement's name sake, "word-faith," presumes that faith is a substance entirely contrary to the teachings of scripture.

Before entering the fragmented theological minds of WoF teachers, one should firmly establish a truly biblical definition of exactly what faith *is*. Knowing the truth is the quintessential position from which one should be able to clearly see error.

Systematic biblical study produces a clear definition of what faith truly is, and how faith is practiced. To begin, the Bible illustrates faith as something which must include two dimensions: belief and resolve. To put it simply, true faith is not simply a mechanically accurate "thinking," but a life changing assurance of that which is not yet realized. Such an understanding of biblical faith is demonstrated clearly in the book of Hebrews. Chapter eleven begins with a concise definition of faith, followed by examples of how faith unfolds in the lives of faithful men.

> ***Hebrews 11:1 (ESV)***
> [1] *Now faith is the assurance of things hoped for, the conviction of things not seen.*

Chapter 6 - Faith: The Omnipotent Entity

The two operative terms in this text, "assurance" and "conviction" both indicate the clear foundation of biblical faith. "Assurance," in the ESV is translated from the Greek term *hypostasis,* a noun referring to a strong confidence and certainty of that which it is aimed. "Conviction" translates from the Greek, *elenchos,* which means "a proof" or "the proving" of something. Thus, faith is something that is not believed half-heartedly or merely intellectually, it is something that is essentially *known and proven* without having to be seen.

While this concise definition gives a cursory understanding of a certain and proven-though-unproven belief as a fundamental element of faith, most of the remainder of Hebrews 11 illustrates what the Bible considers *true faith* after this manner. These illustrations do not equate true belief with someone "thinking" something really hard, or "considering" something as true but rather, for someone to believe something so fully that he is willing to base his resolve upon it.

In illustration of the principle, verse four notes,

> *Hebrews 11:4 (ESV)*
> *⁴ By faith Abel offered to God a more acceptable sacrifice than Cain, through which he was commended as righteous, God commending him by accepting his gifts. And through his faith, though he died, he still speaks.*

Abel is considered faithful not because of his cognitive reasoning abilities, but because his faith was life-changing in the sense that he abided by it and acted upon it. He truly believed, therefore he *offered* a better sacrifice.

Similarly, in verse 17,

> *Hebrews 11:17 (ESV)*
> *¹⁷ By faith Abraham, when he was tested, offered up*

> *Isaac, and he who had received the promises was in the act of offering up his only son,*

Abraham, likewise, was not credited as faithful because of his thinking but rather because of his *demonstration* of faith. Abraham "offered up Isaac." It is clear in retrospect that God was testing Abraham's faith by asking him to offer Isaac in sacrifice. But the question must be asked, "Was Abraham found faithful for *thinking* God meant what he said, or for being willing to live as though what God had said was true?" Verse 17 clearly states the answer; "by faith Abraham...offered up Isaac."

While belief is an essential element of faith, the full test and manifestation of faith is that it is certain; so certain that one's resolve is affected and the proof of faith is demonstrated. Beyond a static consideration of something as true, true faith is exemplified in scripture by those who possess an articulate change of mind, heart or direction because of it. James notes contrarily,

> ***James 2:19 (ESV)***
> [19] *You believe that God is one; you do well. Even the demons believe—and shudder!*

The demons believe academically in one God, but they lacked the resolve to follow through on such. Thus, they were condemned. While their static understanding concerning God is true, their actions are quite contrary.

While this examination of biblical faith is very cursory, it is sufficient at this point to demonstrate a very essential principle regarding biblical faith: *it has an object.* Faith does not exist outside of a solemn, life-altering conviction *of something.* One has faith *in God.* Or, one has faith *that his car will start.* Faith, by its definition and nature, must be attributed to something else in existence. Faith has an object, much like love or hate. One does not simply "love," but one loves *something.* One does not

Chapter 6 - Faith: The Omnipotent Entity

simply believe, but one has an object of that belief, which becomes the object of one's faith when he resolves to trust that belief. One may believe in Santa Clause, alien life forms or the Jolly Green Giant. But, one does not simply "believe" without an object of that belief. One believes *in something*. Faith is not an essence unto itself, but is invested in an additional component. As rudimentary as this statement may seem, the WoF definition of faith miserably fails at this basic level of comprehension.

The WoF doctrine teaches that faith has *no object*, but that it is an entity of its own. To put it in the words of Ken Copeland, "faith is a force."

WoF teachers teach that faith is likened to a magic potion. When applied, this "force" of faith brings about miraculous things. Understand: it is not *God as the object of one's faith* which brings about miraculous things, but *faith itself*.

Kenneth Copeland, seemingly having taken the sheriff's position from the late Kenneth Hagin, is a leading proponent of the "force of faith" perjury. He repeatedly asserts,

> "Faith is a spiritual force....It is substance. Faith has the ability to effect natural substance."[20]

In this statement, Copeland completely ignores the essence of faith which a six year old can comprehend: that faith has an *object*. Faith is based *on something*, and biblical faith has God as its object. Yet, in Copeland's world view, faith "is substance" without an object. Copeland proclaims,

---

[20] **Kenneth Copeland** *Forces of the Recreated Human Spirit* (Fort Worth: Kenneth Copeland Ministries, 1982), 8.

> "The force of gravity...makes the law of gravity work...this force of faith...makes the laws of the spirit world function."[21]

Seemingly lacking the most basic grasp of abstract thought, Copeland relegates faith to the paradoxical position of being a force in and of itself which "makes the laws of the spirit world function." To that end, faith is like fire, water or any other tangible element. It has essence in and of itself. This outlandish idea is not even remotely similar to the Bible's depiction of faith – *in God*; to do and be as He has spoken.

Had Copeland stopped with his maligning of conventional language alone, one would only consider him delusional. But, he doesn't. In his world, this force of faith is the greatest force in existence, even including the force of the power of almighty God himself. Incredulously, Copeland contends that

> "Faith is God's source of power"
> **Kenneth Copeland** (Freedom From Fear, 1983. p. 12)

God's *source* of power? How foolish we all must be to have thought that God was all-powerful on his own accord! In WoF teaching, there is a substance in existence which is mightier than God, by which God somehow mystically draws his sustenance; the all-powerful force of faith. If one follows this logic to its conclusion, then God is not God. Faith is. For it is faith which is the supposed power source behind what God does. God, therefore, is somehow the beneficiary of this great force, which he harnessed and utilized to do the great things he has done.

---

[21] **Kenneth Copeland** *The Laws of Prosperity* (Fort Worth: Kenneth Copeland Publications, 1974) 18-19

As blasphemous as that idea is, Copeland cannot get enough of it. He continues even to the point of asserting that,

> "Faith was the raw material substance that the Spirit of God used to form the universe."
> **Kenneth Copeland** (Authority of the Believer II, 1987, audiotape #01-0302, side 1)

Exceptionally contrary to scripture, this teaching demands that faith be of a higher essence than God himself. In this view, God apparently promoted himself to his position by his ability to grab ahold of and harness this much greater substance than himself. Such is a smack in the face of the Almighty. The biblical God has no equal, let alone a superior. He has no predecessor from which to draw his essence or his power. He is the alpha and omega; the beginning and the end. HE ALONE is the substance by which the universe was formed. He alone existed when nothing else existed. Such is the entirety of scriptural testimony on the subject. And, in the scripture to have faith is to trust in God alone as one who has power over all things.

Isaiah notes,

> *Isaiah 41:4 (ESV)*
> *⁴ Who has performed and done this, calling the generations from the beginning? I, the LORD, the first, and with the last; I am he.*

To adhere to WoF teaching, one must accept that God has faith in something outside of his own power and that he used it to invoke the creation of all known matter. What, pray tell, would God have faith *in?* One may logically thus conclude that *faith* is that which should be worshiped instead of God. Woefully, such is quite nearly the case in the WoF movement, for the "force of faith" is the confession men are charged to call upon for their needs, rather than God. In this unbiblical crusade, calling out "to faith" is common practice.

Complimenting this convoluted doctrine of faith as a God-trumping force is a counter-doctrine concerning "words" by which the force of faith is to be tamed into submission. "Words," it is taught, are the *containers* of this mythological faith substance.

As noted earlier, WoF teachers draw their false doctrines from one of two sources. Their first choice is to damage scripture; misquoting and misrepresenting it. When that fails, choice two is the aforementioned bogus use of revelation knowledge. In this case, the former was attainable, by the maligning of Hebrews 11:3. Ironically, this verse lies in the very middle of the text which properly was earlier demonstrated to illustrate a proper definition of what faith is. Yet, in the hands of a WoF wordsmith, even what scripture clearly says can be twisted to say the complete opposite.

In verse three of the Hebrews 11 demonstration of faith it is noted,

> ***Hebrews 11:3 (ESV)***
> *³ By faith we understand that the universe was created by the word of God, so that what is seen was not made out of things that are visible.*

This text is clear enough to one who desires to interpret it. It states that we exhibit faith when we understand that God formed the universe by his command. Thus, our understanding comes from faith: "by faith we understand that the universe was formed at God's command...."

In the WoF teachers rendering of the same text, the terms "we understand" are parenthetical. They are completely ignored as being essential to the sentence. By intentionally abusing this text, WoF teachers render it,

Chapter 6 - Faith: The Omnipotent Entity

"by faith (we understand) the universe was formed at God's command...." So, the faith in this text, according to WoF was "the force" of faith. As they hear it, it should more properly be written "we understand that by faith God formed the universe by his command." Of course this completely disregards the context and framing of every other sentence in the text. Every "by faith" assertion in the text speaks to an action which illustrates the faith of an individual *toward God*. By faith, Abel offered. By faith, Noah built. By faith Sarah conceived. By faith Abraham obeyed. And, by faith, "we understand." Using the WoF misrepresentation of the text, one may also be inclined to believe that faith is released by offering, building, conceiving, etc. But, of course, only verse three is to be considered in the falsifying of the doctrine.

In their warping of the phrase, it becomes faith which formed the universe. And, in this abuse of scripture, God's *word* is that which releases his faith; "by faith... the universe was formed at God's *command*." Thus, a doctrine of words – as the containers of faith – is born. God speaks words, releasing the force of faith, and the universe is formed.

Lest anyone think this work is attempting to misrepresent WoF doctrine on the subject, consider the following quotes:

> "Now, God used faith substance to make everything that He made ... in every one of those words they were filled with faith substance, because words are nothing but containers ... every time God speaks, He can't help but to speak words that are filled with faith ... God's guts are called faith stuff ... Everything in Him is faith. What's in His heart is faith ... if you were to cut God open, you'd see nothing but faith. Every time He

opens His mouth now, He automatically fills those words with His faith material." [22]

"God did not create the world out of nothing, He used the Force of His Faith."[23]

The logical conclusion of this myth yields the WoF doctrine of words being the containers which wield the force of faith. This idea is presented as "spiritual law." Words are said to simply *have the power of faith* within them; not only for God, but for *anyone* to use. In this fantasy, all of humanity has the power of the force of faith at their fingertips; even pagans!

"Words create pictures, and pictures in your mind create words. And then the words come back out your mouth....And when that spiritual force comes out it is going to give substance to the image that's on the inside of you. Aw, that's that visualization stuff! Aw, that's that New Age! No, New Age is trying to do this; and they'd get somewhat results out of it because this is spiritual law, brother." [24]

Copeland concludes that even New Agers (eastern mystics) get results from visualizing and speaking faith-filled words, because it is a spiritual law. In this case, the force of faith is not relegated to serve God alone, but anyone who has this secret knowledge. Indeed, according to Benny Hinn, even the very incarnation of Christ was the result of the force of faith being uttered by the prophets.

---

[22] **Creflo Dollar** *Changing Your World* broadcast (September 20, 1998)

[23] **Kenneth Copeland** (Spirit, Soul, & Body, #01-0601, Tape #1)

[24] **Kenneth Copeland** (Believer's Voice of Victory, TBN, March 28, 1991)

Chapter 6 - Faith: The Omnipotent Entity

> "The Bible says the prophets spoke the Word not knowing what they were saying. But 4000 years passed when the Word became a human being and walked and talked and moved. The spoken Word became a human being. The spoken Word became flesh. The spoken Word got legs on, arms, eyes, hair, a body. And He was no longer saying, 'Thus sayeth the Lord.' He was saying, 'I say unto you.' The Word that was spoken through the lip of prophets was now walking on the seashore of Galilee"[25]
>
> Jesus existed only as an image in the heart of God, until such time as the prophets of the Old Testament could positively confess Jesus into existence through their constant prophecies. [26]

In this conjecture, Hinn and Copeland not only credit the Old Testament prophets with the incarnation of Christ, but Hinn misuses John 1 to supposedly support his theory. In noting that the "word became flesh," Hinn eludes to that chapter:

> ***John 1:1-3 (ESV)***
> *[1] In the beginning was the Word, and the Word was with God, and the Word was God. [2] He was in the beginning with God. [3] All things were made through him, and without him was not any thing made that was made.*

Ironically, this chapter does not support his view at all, but refutes it! Verse 1 clearly states "the Word was God" and verse 3 states "all things were made through him." There is no mention of the word of faith – only the Word

---

[25] **Benny Hinn** (TBN December 15 1990)

[26] **Kenneth Copeland** *The Power of the Tongue* (Fort Worth: Kenneth Copeland Publications, 1997) 8-10

Apostasy! | 65

that *was God.* Verse 14 clarifies further, using Hinn's mis-applied quote:

> ***John 1:14 (ESV)***
> *[14] And the Word became flesh and dwelt among us, and we have seen his glory, glory as of the only Son from the Father, full of grace and truth.*

In John 1, "the Word" refers not to the spoken word of the prophets, but of God himself, in the person of Jesus Christ. The Word of John 1 is personified in Christ. It is not an impersonal force of faith, a "substance" that was the result of the advent, but the person of Jesus Christ, pre-existent of all creation. How treacherous to credit the incarnation of the pre-existent Christ to the word-faith of the prophets! If such a doctrine were true, then it was Isaiah who sent God's only son to die for men, not God himself. Perhaps we should pray and thank "faith," Isaiah or Jeremiah for sending Christ to the earth to provide our atonement?

Sadly, this "Word of Faith" doctrine is embraced wholeheartedly among the followers of these false shepherds. And this "word of faith" is the hook for the marketplace where such doctrines are to be preached. Since it is taught that one's spoken word can release the force of faith, there is literally no end to the possibilities of what one's confession can yield. Anything one's heart desires can be released from thought to reality by the mere speaking in faith of words. As Copeland defines it,

> "You have the same creative faith and ability on the inside of you that God used when he created the heavens and the earth."[27]

---

[27] **Kenneth Copeland** (Inner Image of the Covenant, side 2) Audio

Chapter 6 - Faith: The Omnipotent Entity

Congratulations, WoF proponent. You have a mouth. You can release the same force that God released when he created you. Likewise eastern mystics, pagans and atheists (who also have mouths) are able to utter words as faith-containers to produce their own creations outside of the work of God in Christ. Such an affirmation relegates the entirety of the life and ministry of Christ as purposeless and a product of human projection. This is not Christian doctrine. It is not Christianity at all.

Yet, this doctrine has become the modus operandi of the entire marketing strategy of WoF life. Simply put, everyone wants something. Now, the false teacher has a means to sell it to them. It matters not if one wants money, fame, power or healing. Through this faith doctrine, literally any desire of one's heart is accessible by a faith incantation. Marilyn Hickey notes,

> "Say to your body, 'You're whole, body! Why, you just function so beautifully and so well. Why, body, you never have any problems. You're a strong, healthy body.' Or speak to your leg, or speak to your foot, or speak to your neck, or speak to your back; and once you have spoken and believe that you have received, and don't go back on it. Speak to your wife, speak to your husband, speak to your circumstances; and speak faith to them to create in them and God will create what you are speaking."

> "What do you need? Start creating it. Start speaking about it. Start speaking it into being. Speak to your billfold. Say, "You big, thick billfold full of money." Speak to your checkbook. Say, "You, checkbook, you. You've never been so prosperous since I owned you.

You're just jammed full of money."[28]

In Hickey's world, at least God seems to have a role in it. She notes that "God will create what you are speaking." Perhaps she missed the memo proclaiming that God is only a faith-user, but she clearly has accepted the word-power tenet of the technique. Healing, beauty, physical strength, money and prosperity have never been so easy to acquire. It merely requires that one speak positive confessions into existence. It makes one wonder why so many destitute, sick and injured people continue to flock to hear these wolves preach. Why have they not all been freed? Why are they still poor? Why do we see them leaving such events in the same wheelchairs they arrived in? Are they unable to speak? Sadly, instead of finding riches, they give what little they have to the false shepherd as "faith offerings" in the hopes of obtaining their counterfeit miracle. And instead of finding healing, they are accused of lacking the necessary faith to deserve health.[29] Even in the shallow end of the WoF pool, the teaching is the same. T.D. Jakes and Joel Osteen, both considered to be "not quite as bad" as their colleagues in this shell game, are full-fledged proponents of the same lies.

> "It's what you say to yourself that gets you healed. If you say that you won't be healed, you won't be healed. If you say that you are broke, you will stay broke. Oh! But I came to serve notice on the Devil. The Bible says, 'The power of life and death is in the tongue.' Slap somebody and say, 'You better speak to

---

[28] **Marilyn Hickey** (Claim Your Miracles audiotape #186, side 2) Audio

[29] See Chapter 12

> yourself.' "[30]
>
> "You can cancel out God's plan by speaking negative words. God works by laws" [31]
>
> Fear is a force just like faith is a force. If you give into fear and start to dwell on that junk and start to act on it, that fear can actually bring things to pass just like faith can bring things to pass. Job said, 'the thing I greatly feared came upon me." [32]

Faith-filled words are the instrument by which all of man's needs may be met in this tradition. Gone is the dependence upon God for one's daily provision. Gone are the acceptance of his judgment for sin, the consequences of uncontrolled spending and the need to rely on God's direction for life. The WoF proponent is proclaimed to be in control of his own destiny through the power of his tongue.

The quotes in this chapter are a mere foreshadowing of the great heights which these teachers claim the word of faith can take those who speak it. And, sadly, a mere foundation stone upon which an entire false systematized theology was laid. The disclosure of their apostasy has only just begun.

---

[30] **T.D. Jakes**, *Seize The Moment, Woman Thou Art Loosed* (Atlanta: TD Jakes Ministries, 2000) Video

[31] **Joel Osteen**, (Speaking Faith Filled Words, Tape # 223) Daystar Television, May 2, 2004

[32] **Joel Osteen**, Sermon, VL-007, April 30, 2000

Chapter 7 - Elevating Man to Godhood

Upon the inclusion of one faulty doctrine, as noted earlier, a domino effect is put into place that modifies one's entire systematized theological system. Once it is presumed that man can "speak" anything he wants into existence – by the power of the force of faith – then the status of man is necessarily changed from the biblical position of being dependent on God to a posture of self-sufficiency. At the point in the fable when man becomes the commander of the very power God used to create the universe the tables are necessarily turned on the Deity/Subject relationship. The first domino to fall in the WoF theological system is that man's nature becomes elevated; for he now is presumed to have at his disposal the very finger of God's power: full access to the force of faith.

This new anthropology has since been retroactively injected into the biblical account from the beginning. According to WoF creation doctrine, which incidentally was developed *after* the inclusion of the erroneous faith force farce, God made the heavens, earth and man in a completely new and extra-biblical context. Their claim is that God's intention with man was not to create a subjugate being who would know and worship God, but that He would create another god like himself in man, and give man the same powers that God possessed. Benny Hinn claims,

Chapter 7 - Elevating Man to Godhood

> *"God came to earth and touched a piece of dust and turned it into a God."*[33]

As strange as that sounds, it is the confession of WoF leaders through and through: Adam was a *reproduction* of God. Creflo Dollar concedes,

> "I'm going to have to reproduce Myself; like I'm God up here in heaven. I'm going to make Me a god and put Myself in the physical body so that he can guard the earth and keep out all intruders in the earth ... Now that gives us a little insight on why God wanted a god on the earth like He was God in heaven ... When God made Adam all He did was make an exact imprint of Himself. He duplicated Himself ... If you eat of this fruit, you will be like God. What's the problem? He's already like God. He was already like God."[34]

This mythological creation of WoF teachers presumes that man was actually God's equal in every manner. Hagin Senior, in his own understanding of the necessity of the Word-Faith doctrine to impact biblical anthropology, had already sewn the seed of this doctrine. He notes,

> "[Man] was created on terms of equality with God, and he could stand in God's presence without any consciousness of inferiority...God made us as much like Himself as possible...He made us the same class of being that He is Himself...Man lived in the realm of God. He lived on terms equal with God...[The] believer

---

[33] **Benny Hinn** (TBN broadcast, Dec 1, 1990)

[34] **Creflo Dollar** (Our equality with God Through Righteousness January 21, 2001)

is called Christ...That's who we are; we're Christ"[35]

As the WoF myth continues, this man-god, Adam, had the fullness of the godhead within him. He had super-human powers and could do amazing things (which the Bible has failed to mention). Hinn claims,

> "Adam was a super-being when God created him. I don't know whether people know this, but he was the first superman that really ever lived. First of all, the Scriptures declare clearly that he had dominion over the fowls of the air, the fish of the sea--which means he used to fly. Of course, how can he have dominion over the birds and not be able to do what they do? The word 'dominion' in the Hebrew clearly declares that if you have dominion over a subject that you do everything that subject does. In other words, that subject, if it does something you cannot do, you don't have dominion over it. I'll prove it further. Adam not only flew, he flew to space. He was--with one thought he would be on the moon."[36]

In this case, Hinn builds his understanding of Adam's purported flying, space traveling and moon-jumping from a single term in the Hebrew text. Referring to Genesis 1:26, using the term "dominion," Hinn creates a gross misrepresentation of the creation of humanity. The text in question states,

> ***Genesis 1:26 (ESV)***
> *²⁶ Then God said, "Let us make man in our image, after our likeness. And let them have dominion over the fish of the sea and over the birds of the heavens and over*

---

[35] **Kenneth Hagin, Sr.** *Zoe: The God-Kind of Life* (Tulsa: Faith Library, 1989) 35-36, 41

[36] **Benny Hinn** (Praise the Lord, TBN December 26, 1991)

the livestock and over all the earth and over every creeping thing that creeps on the earth."

The first error of this doctrine is that the statement "Let us make man in our image" does not relegate man to God's status. In fact, this statement actually consigns man to something *essentially lower* that God, not equal. The phrase "let us create" relegates man to the position of a *creation*, while God is pre-existent and eternal; having no beginning and certainly no moment of creation. Essentially, simple logic dictates that which is created must be lower than that which is created. Scripture concurs, as it relegates man to being lower than the angels, who themselves are created beings.[37]

The second error is the ridiculous idea that Hinn, from the term "dominion," can fabricate Adam into a flying, moon-jumping super being. Hinn's statement, "The word 'dominion' in the Hebrew clearly declares that…you do everything that subject does," is simply outrageous. The Hebrew term in question is *rada*. It means "to rule" or "to subjugate." Simply stated, the term means to have administrative oversight or to reign over. There is absolutely *nothing* inherent in the term even hinting that the one in dominion has the same abilities as that which he rules. The term occurs 27 times in the Old Testament, and never does it indicate that abilities of the subject are transferred to the ruler. Hinn, to be blunt, is simply abusing his perceived authority over his followers and taking advantage of their ignorance of the Hebrew language to support his false claim.

The third error is, of course, the idea that Adam could fly *into space and land on the moon.* Even if Hinn were

---

[37] Psalm 8:5

Apostasy! | 73

speaking truthfully about the meaning of *rada*, there is no creature on the earth – under the dominion of Adam – that could fly to the moon. At this point it seems that he is literally getting caught up in his own propagandizing.

As a side note, another clear indicator of the error of Hinn's claim is the fact that man's dominion of the earth is never taken away. As such, if dominion meant that Adam could fly to the moon, then we should all be able to do as such, for man's dominion over the earth was given and never taken away. It remains an inherent trait of man's stead in creation. The psalmist notes,

> ***Psalm 8:5-8 (ESV)***
> [5] *Yet you have made him a little lower than the heavenly beings and crowned him with glory and honor.*
> [6] *You have given him dominion over the works of your hands; you have put all things under his feet,*
> [7] *all sheep and oxen, and also the beasts of the field,*
> [8] *the birds of the heavens, and the fish of the sea, whatever passes along the paths of the seas.*

Such dominion over the creation was never revoked. Man remains in dominion – in the true biblical sense – over all other created beings. Yet, in order to fly to the moon he had to invest thousands of years of scientific knowledge and millions of dollars in capital to create a machine to get him there. Indeed, man took possession of the materials of the earth and flew to the moon, but he did not do so "with one thought."

This fallacy of man's equality with God comes directly from Satan's own repertoire, as it was Satan who began the propagation of that particular false theology. Even in Genesis 3 when he notes "you will be like God," Satan is tempting man with Satan's own evil desire to be like God. To be like God is the ultimate goal of sin. It is to be without restraint, without rule, without boundaries and most of all without accountability to a creator. Such is absolutely *not* a condition granted to man in the creative order. Man was *not* an exact duplicate of God in human form. That manifestation happened only once, in the person of Jesus Christ.

Building on these myths of humanity, WoF teachers further proclaim that the fall of man hindered Adam's god-status, but that Christ returned man to being a "little god" in his provision of redemption. Copeland is particularly arrogant in such assertions, noting to his audience,

> "You don't have a god in you, you are one" [38]

and,

> "I say this with all respect so that it don't upset you too bad, but I say it anyway. When I read in the Bible where he [Jesus] says, 'I Am,' I just smile and say, 'Yes, I am, too!'" [39]

Unless he repents, Copeland will spend eternity refuting his own testimony. Such falsification of man's god-status, presumed re-stated in Christ, has brought the WoF leadership to the worst possible condition of equating themselves with Jesus! Copeland haughtily mocks Christ in his assertion that,

> "Jesus is no longer the only begotten Son of God." [40]

---

[38] **Kenneth Copeland** (The Force of Love, 1987, audiotape #02-0028, side 1)

[39] **Kenneth Copeland** (Believer's Voice of Victory, TBN July 9, 1987)

[40] **Kenneth Copeland** *Now We Are In Christ Jesus* (Fort Worth: Kenneth Copeland Publications, 1980) 24

Apostasy! | 75

WoF doctrine teaches that salvation is the reinstating of man's deific position with God. The shocking assertion of this teaching is that the believer, upon their salvation in Christ, literally becomes a "little god" and a perfect incarnation of God – just as Christ, the only begotten son, was. The egotism of such a position is staggering, but remains a fundamental tenet of WoF doctrine. Even from earlier days, Hagin touted this very myth, noting,

> "You are as much the incarnation of God as Jesus Christ was...the believer is as much an incarnation as was Jesus of Nazareth".[41]

Hinn goes so far as to denigrate John 1, the chapter which highlights the superiority of Christ in creation, by noting,

> "When you were born again the Word was made flesh in you. You are everything He was and everything He is and ever He shall be. Don't say,' I have.' Say, ' I am, I am, I am, I am, I am."[42]

Thus, man is hereby granted by the WoF teacher an equal footing with Christ himself. He is "everything (Christ) was…is and ever He shall be." Such foolishness is beyond the capacity of a legitimate believer in Christ. These men are impostors of the highest order; slandering even Christ as a being of no greater value than themselves.

Paul Crouch, the founder of Trinity Broadcasting Network, not only tolerates such foolishness, but willingly contributes to its proliferation. Crouch concurs,

> "He [God] doesn't even draw a distinction between

---

[41] **Kenneth Hagin, Sr.** "Word Of Faith" December, 1980, p. 14

[42] **Benny Hinn** ("Our Position in Christ #2 -- The Word Made Flesh" 1991, audiotape #A031190-2, side 2)

Chapter 7 - Elevating Man to Godhood

> Himself and us. . . . You know what else that's settled, then, tonight? This hue and cry and controversy that has been spawned by the Devil to try and bring dissension within the body of Christ that we are gods. I am a little god! . . . I have His name. I'm one with Him. I'm in covenant relation. I am a little god! Critics, be gone!"[43]

The WoF "little gods" doctrine is nothing more than a repackaging of Satan's original sin. Isaiah notes,

> ***Isaiah 14:12-14 (ESV)***
> *[12] "How you are fallen from heaven, O Day Star, son of Dawn! How you are cut down to the ground, you who laid the nations low!*
> *[13] You said in your heart, 'I will ascend to heaven; above the stars of God I will set my throne on high; I will sit on the mount of assembly in the far reaches of the north;*
> *[14] I will ascend above the heights of the clouds; I will make myself like the Most High.'*

The teaching of man's elevation to god-status is an essential element of WoF systematic theology. It is from this premise that the supporters of these wicked teachers can be shaped into an understanding of the rest of the theological story. From a god-status, man is in control and can do as God did, using the force of faith to create one's own reality and shape one's own future. The end result, according to these teachers, puts man as sovereign over his own circumstances, being an incarnation of Christ, with authority to rule one's own life.

> "You have the same creative faith and ability on the inside of you that God used when he created the

---

[43] **Paul Crouch** (*Praise the Lord* Broadcast, TBN, July 7, 1986)

heavens and the earth."[44]

The scriptures teach a distinctly different truth about man from the Word of Faith heresy. Man, being a creation of God, is utterly subordinate to God, and will remain so for all eternity. Man *is not a little god.* In fact, the true God claimed on numerous occasions the *he alone* is God, and that all other supposed gods are mute, powerless and non-existent. The Lord proclaims in Isaiah 43:10, "··· Before me no god was formed, nor shall there be any after me." He concurs in Isaiah 45:21, "···there is no other god besides me, a righteous God and a Savior; there is none besides me."

Clearly God does not consider mankind to be "little gods." It is God's declaration that there are no other gods but him. Furthermore, God proclaims that his followers *belong* to him and that he rules over them.[45] Man is in no position to *bargain* with God, or to share God's stature. Man's life was written by God before one day of it began. God declares adamantly in Isaiah 42:8 that "I will not give my glory to another or my praise to idols."

It is the epitome of Satanic arrogance for a man to equate himself with God. Such are what men like David Koresh and Jose Luis de Miranda are condemned for by the Christian community. Anyone who claims to be Christ demonstrates nothing short of demonic influence which propagates Satan's original quest of a god-status. How ironic that the men of the largest purported Christian television station on earth regularly make the exact same claims without a hint of rebuke or apparently even a notice of incongruity from their faithful followers.

---

[44] **Kenneth Copeland** (Inner Image of the Covenant, side 2)

[45] Psalm 100:3, Psalm 139:15-16

Such is the result of one bad doctrine gone amuck and affecting others. If man has power over the mythological force of faith – the same power God used to create the earth – then man must necessarily be elevated to a god-status; for he has the very power of God in his hands and at his command.

Chapter 8 - The Demotion of God

Necessarily, the next domino to fall is that of Theology proper: the doctrine of God the Father. If man is elevated to a god-status, then God is necessarily demoted to a plane consistent with that of man. You cannot theologically elevate man to God without demoting God to the status of man in the same move. My hope would be that the average attender of a WoF church would maintain that such could never happen. Surely no one would suggest that God is anything less than He claims to be in scripture: omnipotent, omniscient and sovereign over all creation. Yet, all three of these historically preserved biblical attributes are seriously compromised by the WoF movement in order to make room for the force of faith farce.

The essence of God's demotion is taught by the WoF to be the results of Adam's sin. The postulate is that God, making Adam in his likeness as a "little god" also gave Adam the ability to give away the earth. They claim that God gave the earth to Adam and Adam gave it to Satan as the after-effect of Adam's sin. In this bizarre theological twist God literally "lost" the earth to Satan in a weird power play involving humanity. Accordingly, God then had no power to invest in the earth. He had become an outsider to his own creation. Copeland explains,

> "The Bible says that God gave this earth to the sons of men ... and when [Adam] turned and gave that dominion to Satan, look where it left God. It left Him

> on the outside looking in ... He had no legal right to do anything about it, did He? ... He had injected Himself illegally into the earth -- what Satan had intended for Him to do was to fall for it -- pull off an illegal act and turn the light off in God, and subordinate God to himself ... He intended to get God into such a trap that He couldn't get out."[46]

First of all, the Bible never says that God gave the earth to the sons of men. The phrase "sons of men" does not appear in the creation account at all, but rather in the account of the evil which prevailed upon the earth prior to the flood in Genesis 6. Once again, we have an example of a WoF teacher simply "making up" scripture on the fly. Can we have a chapter and verse, Ken? That is, after all, how a real preacher does it: he studies the text, exegetes it and delivers it expressly as possible. Copeland can't afford to do this on this point, as the Bible does not say what he wants it to.

Neither does the scripture say that God "gave" the earth to Adam. It merely says that he assigned dominion to Adam over the earth and the earth's creatures. Never does such a sentiment suggest a change in ownership of the earth. Man's dominion over the earth was a stewardship likened to a businessman putting a general manager over a factory. Ownership never changes. The source of power never changes. The owner will always be sovereign over the function of the company through his manager.

God, by assigning man to a position of dominion over the earth, is in fact asserting his ownership of the earth in such a designation. If God gave the earth to man, man would have dominion by default. But such is not what

---

[46] **Kenneth Copeland** (What Happened from the Cross to the Throne, 1990, audiotape #02-0017)

God did. Contrarily, the Bible is rather clear that God has not given away the earth *to anyone*. Paul, quoting Psalm 24:1, notes,

> ***1 Corinthians 10:26 (ESV)***
> *[26] For "the earth is the Lord's, and the fullness thereof."*

Moses spoke on the subject, stating,

> ***Deuteronomy 10:14 (ESV)***
> *[14] Behold, to the LORD your God belong heaven and the heaven of heavens, the earth with all that is in it.*

Where is this reference to God's losing of the earth in scripture? Not only is the postulate that "God lost the earth" ridiculous and unbiblical, true biblical content further notes after Adam's sin it was God - not Satan or Adam - who redefined the condition of earth as a result of sin. It was God who said to Adam,

> ***Genesis 3:17 (ESV)***
> *[17] ... "Because you have listened to the voice of your wife and have eaten of the tree of which I commanded you, 'You shall not eat of it,' cursed is the ground because of you; in pain you shall eat of it all the days of your life;*

According to Copeland, "[God was] left on the outside looking in." How, then, did God curse the Earth? If God "had no legal right to do anything about it" then who exactly fulfilled God's curse? Did Satan curse the earth at God's request? This postulate not only lacks scriptural validation, but also common sense.

Furthermore, the idea that there is some legal system which relegates God to a subordinate is utterly laughable to anyone who knows the God of scripture. It is God who is the ultimate source of *all law*. There is no law above him. There is no law-giver besides him. Who exactly is the author, judge and enforcer of Copeland's nonsensical "legal rights" that God supposedly lost? Perhaps the "force of faith" is this superpower making rules over God's head? Perhaps it is Copeland himself, as he certainly seems to believe in his own authority over our Lord.

Even children in a Bible teaching church know better than such foolishness. Scripture teaches rightly that God is not consigned to any power but his own. Job notes,

> **Job 23:13 (ESV)**
> [13] But he is unchangeable, and who can turn him back? What he desires, that he does.

The God of scripture has no law above him. He is unregulated. He does what He desires; and it is His very desire that establishes all law. The Psalmist continues,

> **Psalm 33:11 (ESV)**
> [11] The counsel of the LORD stands forever, the plans of his heart to all generations.

Solomon concurs,

> **Proverbs 19:21 (ESV)**
> [21] Many are the plans in the mind of a man, but it is the purpose of the LORD that will stand.

By what audacity does a WoF teacher maintain that God is at the mercy of some unwritten legal system? And, unwritten it remains, for at no point does the Bible even hint that God is subject to Copeland's "spiritual law."

In fact, *every single statement* of Copeland's previous quote is utterly lacking in *any* biblical evidence. The entire notion is another made up doctrine. Of such, Jeremiah notes,

> **Jeremiah 14:14 (ESV)**
> [14] And the LORD said to me: "The prophets are prophesying lies in my name. I did not send them, nor did I command them or speak to them. They are

Apostasy! | 83

prophesying to you a lying vision, worthless divination, and the deceit of their own minds.

But Copeland is not alone in this charade. He, being the mantle-boy for Hagin's WoF dream, is mimicked and repeated by every other huckster in the game. Frederick Price is fully on board with him, noting:

> "Adam, as I said, gave it [the earth] away to the serpent, to the Devil. As a result of it, he got his behind kicked out of the garden. He went out of Eden, out of the garden. He began to wander around, and he has troubles from day one. Now God was out of the business. God was out of the earth realm. God had no more stock in this earth realm. No more. None at all. Nothing He could do. Not a thing in the world He could do. . . .The only way God could get back into this earth realm, He had to have an invitation."[47]

Price obviously has the same Bible as Copeland, but a very different one from the rest of us. I can't seem to find any of these nifty doctrines in my 20-something translations on hand. But, Price clearly is a team player. He follows the party line almost verbatim. Indeed, it does appear that God is "out of the business" as far as these men are concerned. He is certainly not in theirs.

It is interesting that Price notes Adam "got his behind kicked out of the garden." By whom, one wonders, was his behind kicked? If God has lost control, should one suppose Price is indicating that Satan kicked Adam out of the Garden of Eden? If God has lost control, and no longer owns the earth, why then does scripture say,

---

[47] **Frederick K.C. Price** (Ever Increasing Faith, TBN, May 1, 1992, audiotape #PR11)

> **Genesis 3:23-24 (ESV)**
> ²³ *therefore the LORD God sent him out from the garden of Eden to work the ground from which he was taken.*
> ²⁴ *He drove out the man, and at the east of the garden of Eden he placed the cherubim and a flaming sword that turned every way to guard the way to the tree of life.*

Clearly, God is still in control. It is He who banished man from Eden. It is He who placed cherubim to guard it. It is He who is in control today, as He has always been and always will be.

Yet, in the warped minds of WoF doctrinal architects, God's authority had been diminished and reassigned to none other than Satan himself. In accordance with God's loss of control on earth came his utter dependence on man to restore his authority once again. According to these teachers, God cannot act in the earth realm outside of man's invitation and enabling. Price explains,

> The only way God could get back into this earth realm, He had to have an invitation. Ha-hah! He had to have an invitation. And so, God looked around--saw different men, saw Noah, saw different ones. He gave them a few instructions. They did what He said. So and so and so and so. But, finally, He got to a point where He had His plan ready for operation. And He saw a man named Abraham."[48]

Thus, the story goes that God made a special deal with Abraham. He promised Abraham riches in exchange for Abraham giving God permission to work in the earth. Through Abraham came Christ and through Christ came

---

[48] **Frederick K.C. Price** (Ever Increasing Faith, TBN, May 1, 1992, audiotape #PR11)

our ability today to give God permission to work in the earth. Of all the ins and outs of the system, one thing is clear: God is not in control in the earth according to the WoF system. As Copeland noted earlier,

> "The Bible says that God gave this earth to the sons of men ...and when [Adam] turned and gave that dominion to Satan"[49]

Hinn proclaims that even today, as God's covenant people, we- through the speaking of the Word of Faith – allow God to work in the earth.

> "...the anointing is dependent upon my words. God will not move unless I say it. Why? because He has made us coworkers with Him. He set things up that way."[50]

Thus, God, being utterly out of control, must be granted the privilege of influencing his creation by none other than man who is merely a part of that creation.

> "God had no avenue of lasting faith or moving in the earth. He had to have covenant with somebody. He had to be invited in, in other words, or He couldn't come. God is on the outside looking in. In order to have any say so in the earth, He's going to have to be in agreement with a man here." [51]

Ultimately, then, the pendulum lands to man being in control in this convoluted doctrine. It is man's control, of course, which best fits the purposes of these teachers.

---

[49] **Kenneth Copeland** (What Happened from the Cross to the Throne, 1990, audiotape #02-0017)

[50] **Benny Hinn** *The Anointing* (Nashville: Thomas Nelson, 1992) 82

[51] **Kenneth Copeland** (God's Covenants With Man II, 1985, audiotape #01-4404, side 1)

Chapter 8 - The Demotion of God

Thus, through God's covenant with Abraham he was given an agreement by which he could once again have a say in the earth realm. Skipping to modernity, Abraham's blessings are now presumed to be passed on to every believer in Christ, so that God now is only able to move when Christians enable him. Such enablement, of course, must come from the confession of the Word of Faith by one who believes in it. Paul Yonggi Cho notes,

> "You create the presence of Jesus with your mouth ... He is bound by your lips and by your words ... Remember that Christ is depending upon you and your spoken word to release His presence."[52]

The end result of this ridiculous creed is not only that man is a little god, but that God is a little man, being literally forced into action by the utterances of humanity. According to Cho, God "is bound by your lips and your words." This false revelation itself creates a contradiction in the WoF theology. Is it the force of faith which responds to man's utterance, or is it God himself?

Copeland seems to believe whichever way is most productive for his cause. In most circumstances he affirms that,

> "Words are spiritual containers,"[53]

and that the

> "force of faith is released by words."[54]

---

[52] **Paul Yonggi (David) Cho** *The Fourth Dimension* (Alachua: Bridge-Logos Publishers, Vol.1, 1979) 83

[53] **Kenneth Copeland** *Forces of the Recreated Human Spirit* (Fort Worth: Kenneth Copeland Ministries, 1982) 15; cf. 14)

[54] **Kenneth Copeland** (Authority of the Believer II, 1987, audiotape #01-0302, side 1)

Clearly he believes that it is the "force of faith" which acts, rather than God. This force is, after all, the very power WoF doctrine declares that God used to create the universe. We, as covenant enablers of God's work in the earth, enable this magic power by visualizing and releasing these word-containers of faith. Copeland further explains that,

> "Words create pictures, and pictures in your mind create words. And then the words come back out your mouth....And when that spiritual force comes out it is going to give substance to the image that's on the inside of you. Aw, that's that visualization stuff! Aw, that's that New Age! No, New Age is trying to do this; and they'd get somewhat results out of it because this is spiritual law, brother." [55]

So, apparently Christ-optional, mankind has access to the "spiritual law" of having visualized faith words to give creative substance. In this scenario, God is on the outside looking in, and man alone has the power to give faith-words to get God's work done.

However, if the idea that some force other than God is in control makes you uncomfortable, Copeland also teaches that *God will respond personally* to your commands, rather than the force of faith. Out of the other side of his mouth he notes the alternative:

> "As a believer, you have a right to make commands in the name of Jesus. Each time you stand on the Word, you are commanding God to a certain extent because

---

[55] **Kenneth Copeland** *Believer's Voice of Victory* broadcast, TBN, March 28, 1991)

it is His Word." [56]

Thus, you have the power to "command God" in the name of Jesus. (Is this scenario not a kingdom divided against itself?) It seems that WoF elementary doctrine cares not whether the power being utilized is God, or the force of faith, as long as the individual has full control over the command of both. The end result is of the paradigm is crystal clear: WoF doctrine asserts that YOU can have whatever you wish by properly commanding such with your mouth. Either God will respond – using the Word of Faith – or the Word of Faith will respond, and trump God's influence.

Amid the confusion, what does remain clear is the assertion that God has been demoted and man has been promoted. Man commands, God depends. Man asserts, God yearns. Man is in control, God is out. Such allegations have absolutely *nothing* in common with the God of scripture.

The God of the Bible is neither at a loss for his own power, nor is he commanded of man. It is he, alone, who rules and he alone who is the source of all power. I strongly encourage anyone who is under the indoctrination of a WoF teacher – be it a rock-star TV celebrity or a local church knock-off – to seriously consider the words of God himself on this subject. It is He who loved the world and gave his son for the redemption of sin. It is He who creates, sustains, upholds and commands the entirety of the universe. He is not at the disposal of any man nor does he require any man to give him aid.

---

[56] **Kenneth Copeland** *Our Covenant with God* (Fort Worth: Kenneth Copeland Publications, 1987) 32

His testimony is very different from the testimony of these impostors of his faith. He declares,

> ***Deuteronomy 32:39 (ESV)***
> *^{39} "See now that I, even I, am he, and there is no god beside me; I kill and I make alive; I wound and I heal; and there is none that can deliver out of my hand."*

These are not the words of an incapacitated power. They are not the words of One who needs man's helping hand to get anything done. This God is the source of all power and the recipient of no assistance. It is He of whom it is written,

> ***1 Chronicles 29:11 (ESV)***
> *^{11} Yours, O LORD, is the greatness and the power and the glory and the victory and the majesty, for all that is in the heavens and in the earth is yours. Yours is the kingdom, O LORD, and you are exalted as head above all.*

While Copeland has the audacity to say,

> "God's on the outside looking in. He doesn't have any legal entree into the earth. The thing don't belong to Him. You see how sassy the Devil was in the presence of God in the book of Job? God said, "Where have you been?" Wasn't any of God's business. He [Satan] didn't even have to answer if he didn't want to ... God didn't argue with him a bit! You see, this is the position that God's been in ... Might say, "Well, if God's running things He's doing a lousy job of it." He hadn't been running 'em....." [57]

Job himself, a man who was refined by suffering and who spoke to God personally notes,

---

[57] **Kenneth Copeland** (Image of God in You III, 1989, audiotape #01-1403, side 1)

> **Job 9:12 (ESV)**
> *12 Behold, he snatches away; who can turn him back? Who will say to him, 'What are you doing?'*
>
> **Job 25:2 (ESV)**
> *2 "Dominion and fear are with God; he makes peace in his high heaven.*

And God's answer to Job's trouble was simply,

> **Job 41:11 (ESV)**
> *11 Who has first given to me, that I should repay him? Whatever is under the whole heaven is mine.*

In conclusion, the concepts of God "losing" his creation and being dependent upon man, are utterly unsound both theologically and rationally: Theologically, because scripture never teaches nor even hints at God having lost his foothold on earth nor in all of creation, and rationally because one who loses his control over his creation cannot be rightfully called God, as he will have been usurped by one more powerful than himself. To follow this flat-out postulate to its logical conclusion, God is no longer God at all, but is in fact at the mercy of his creation. And, this supposition is precisely that of the Word of Faith movement's theology: God is not in control on earth. Fred Price arrogantly confirms the status quo of this doctrinal nightmare,

> "Yes! You are in control! So, if man has control, who no longer has it? God." [58]

Indeed, the "little god" doctrine comes full circle in the WoF world view. Man has not only become "like" God, but has trumped God's power entirely, making man fully in control of his own destiny and even the very actions of

---

[58] **Frederick K.C. Price** ("Prayer: Do You Know What Prayer Is ... and How to Pray?" The Word Study Bible, 1990 p. 1178)

God. Satan must be very proud of these men. His original sin has come to full fruition within the walls of the apostate church.

> *Isaiah 14:14 (ESV)*
> *¹⁴ I will ascend above the heights of the clouds; I will make myself like the Most High.'*

WoF teaching has found its niche in the hearts of a corrupt world, as through this illogical set of doctrines sinful man has received what he has always wanted. He presumes himself to be in control, even over the very God which owns him.

Please understand that these teachers are the enemies of Christ. They intentionally malign his Word. Unless they repent they will meet the judgment that Christ's enemies will all succumb to. For such destruction – for many – is the only means by which they will ever come to the truth.

> *Psalm 83:17-18 (ESV)*
> *¹⁷ Let them be put to shame and dismayed forever; let them perish in disgrace,*
> *¹⁸ that they may know that you alone, whose name is the LORD, are the Most High over all the earth.*

Chapter 9 - Atonement Heresy: Kenoticism

As the next several chapters deal with atonement issues, a brief introduction of that term is in order for those who are uncertain. Salvation, in scripture, is a three-fold process. First and foremost is atonement, or *justification.* Justification refers to the canceling of the debt of sin; the forgiveness of man's offense to God. Following justification begins the work of *sanctification.* Sanctification is the work of the Holy Spirit in the life of a believer, freeing him progressively from the power of sin. Lastly, and the full fruition of biblical salvation is *glorification.* Glorification is the state promised to believers in eternity; to be raised with a glorious new body and be completely free from the presence of sin.

"Atonement" refers theologically to the process whereby justification is applied to a sinner's account. Often times when believers speak of "salvation," they are referring specifically of atonement; the purchase of salvation by blood which reconciles a sinner's guilt. In the Old Testament, *Yom Kippur,* or "The Day of Atonement" was the yearly sacrifice for sins whereby the high priest offered blood before the holy of holies in the Temple, or Tabernacle. Yom Kippur is the foreshadowing of the atoning work of Christ. What was done yearly and incompletely in the animal sacrificial system, Christ utterly fulfilled by the presentation of his own blood upon his crucifixion.[59] While Old Testament atonement referred to a temporary and renewable condition, New Testament atonement is a once-for-all transaction whereby a sinner is completely forgiven for sins: past, present and future. In effect, atonement refers to the transaction by which Christ exchanges his death on the cross vicariously for the death owed by sinful man. At the point of atonement, justification is purchased and a sinner begins a new life in Christ.

The Bible claims with no uncertainty that Christ was God incarnate while he was also man. His name was Emmanuel, which means "God with us."[60] The prophets had declared that Messiah *would be God* when he arrived.[61] The disciples and apostles declared that Jesus Christ was God in the flesh.[62] None-the-less, they also noted him to be man. The historic Christian faith has understood a dual nature of Christ as fully God and fully human from the times of the apostles. This doctrine was furthermore confirmed by the Council of Nicaea in 325. Scripture further proclaims that God was both just and the justifier of man, because he provided his own blood through Christ to redeem man from his sins.[63] As such, if Jesus did not have a deific nature in his human incarnation, the gospel message is flawed; for God is the biblical provider of salvation by his own blood through Christ. Trinitarian doctrine, which WoF proponents claim

---

[59] Hebrews 10:1-14

[60] Matthew 1:23

[61] Isaiah 9:6, Jeremiah 23:5-6

[62] John 20:27-28, Romans 9:6

[63] Acts 20:28, Romans 3:26

Apostasy! | 95

to support, demands the full understanding of this principle.

Therein lays the first substantial problem with Word-Faith atonement theory. While most Word of Faith teachers have historically been accurate on atonement issues at some point, they have since apostatized by promoting the continued demotion of God, through the person of Jesus Christ. In short, WoF atonement teachings render Christ imminently discredited in light of historical theology and biblical testimony because they claim that he was not God while he walked the earth.

WoF teachers today hold unwaveringly to a form of kenoticism, which is a doctrine teaching that Jesus emptied himself of his deity when he came to the earth. While kenoticism varies in its forms, the teaching in generality implies that Jesus "gave up" some or all of his God-nature in order to become man at the advent.

While kenoticism is a false theory in itself, the WoF version of it is excessive even within the framework of the previously flawed theology. Normal kenotic theory contends erroneously that Jesus divested himself of certain deific qualities. Typically, those who adhere to kenotic theories maintain that Christ let go of his omniscience or omnipotence in order to become man. Thus, kenotics normally contend that Christ was a little less than full deity while he was on the earth. This is not accurate, as will be observed shortly. However the WoF version of kenotic theory, not to be outdone by more common heretics, goes far beyond the original error of kenoticism. WoF teachers proclaim that Jesus in fact gave up his deity entirely! WoF teachers declare that Christ was not God whatsoever while on the earth, but a man who *was formerly* God, and who *would* be God again.

Chapter 9 - Atonement Heresy: Kenoticism

Ken Copeland reveals such a belief in the statement,

> "'Don't be disturbed when people accuse you of thinking you are God ... They crucified Me for claiming I was God. I didn't claim that I was God; I just claimed that I walked with Him and that He was in Me. Hallelujah! That's what you're doing ...'"[64]

Copeland supports his kenotic theology from - you guessed it - unverified revelation knowledge in the form of one of his many conversations with God concerning things God had failed to mention to Paul, Peter or John. Copeland maintains that Jesus never claimed to be God, but only that he "walked with Him" and that "He was in Me," such as what you and I might claim. Clearly, in Copeland's mind, being God was not a claim of Christ while he walked the earth in human form.

As usual, the problem with Copeland's position is that it is utterly incompatible with scripture. In the book of John, for example, Jesus makes exactly the profession Copeland claims that he didn't.

> *John 10:24-30 (ESV)*
> *[24] So the Jews gathered around him and said to him, "How long will you keep us in suspense? If you are the Christ, tell us plainly."*
> *[25] Jesus answered them, "I told you, and you do not believe. The works that I do in my Father's name bear witness about me,*
> *[26] but you do not believe because you are not part of my flock.*
> *[27] My sheep hear my voice, and I know them, and they follow me.*

---

[64] **Kenneth Copeland** - "Take Time To Pray," Believer's Voice Of Victory 15, 2 (February 1987): 9

> ²⁸ *I give them eternal life, and they will never perish, and no one will snatch them out of my hand.*
> ²⁹ *My Father, who has given them to me, is greater than all, and no one is able to snatch them out of the Father's hand.*
> ³⁰ *I and the Father are one."*

In John 10, Jesus answers a clear question, "If you are the Christ, tell us plainly." Jesus' response was, "I told you, and you do not believe." It was almost as if he were speaking to Copeland himself! Jesus not only told them plainly that he was the Christ, but concluded with, "I and the Father are one," a foundational tenet of Trinitarian theology. Jesus' claim is crystal clear in the text. He *did* claim to be God. And, he declared the reasoning behind the lack of belief of the Jews who heard him: "you do not believe because you are not part of my flock. My sheep hear my voice, and I know them, and they follow me." There could scarcely be a more solid refutation to the WoF position of Christ's lack of deity as a man. But, for the sake of men like Copeland who cannot understand him, he strictly states, "I and the Father are one," leaving no room for doubt as to his meaning.

It is however crystal clear that those present understood Jesus to be calling himself God, as in the very next verse they tried to stone him for that very claim!

> ***John 10:31-33 (ESV)***
> ³¹ *The Jews picked up stones again to stone him.*
> ³² *Jesus answered them, "I have shown you many good works from the Father; for which of them are you going to stone me?"*
> ³³ *The Jews answered him, "It is not for a good work that we are going to stone you but for blasphemy, because you, being a man, make yourself God."*

If the unbelieving Jews who were present understood Jesus' claim to be God, why can't Copeland and other WoF teachers make that connection? The logical answer

Chapter 9 - Atonement Heresy: Kenoticism

is that such doctrine simply stands opposed to what WoF teachers desire to think. Indeed, their theological system intends to demonstrate that man – any man – can live up to the character, power and glory of Christ. As such, they present Jesus to have excused himself of divinity altogether upon his advent. They claim articulately that Jesus left *all* of his deity behind to come to the earth as completely human, but devoid of a divine nature. Dollar challenges,

> If Jesus came as God, then why did God have to anoint Him? If Jesus - see God's already been anointed. If Jesus came as God, then why did God have to anoint Him? Jesus came as a man, that's why it was *legal* to anoint him. God doesn't need anointing, He *is* anointing. Jesus came as a *man*, and at age 30 God is now getting ready to demonstrate to us, and give us an example of what a *man, with the anointing,* can do."[65]

An entire chapter could be written correcting the errors of this simple paragraph. A focal flaw is the obvious conclusion that Dollar believes Christ to have come to earth as a mere man, and only a man. As a meager human, Dollar contends, Christ was given a special anointing of God to "give us an example of what a man, with the anointing, can do." It takes little doctrinal savvy to realize that the term "anoint" does not mean what Dollar and his partners in apostasy think it means. Such is evident from Dollar's question "why did God have to anoint him?"

---

[65] **Creflo Dollar**, *Jesus' Growth into Sonship* Audio, December 8, 15, 2002

To WoF proponents, "anointing" is substance, much like their understanding of faith. They consider anointing to refer to a magic potion of sorts that, when applied, gives special powers to the anointee. Anointing in scripture was commonly demonstrated by a visible sign, such as the application of oil in the case of David being anointed as King.[66] However, such application of the visible sign of oil was not the power behind such anointing. Rather, God's sovereign choice was. David was not anointed King because he got oil on his head, but because God chose him and sent Samuel to make it known. Likewise, Jesus was anointed by merit of his having been the pre-determined, prophesied and sent One of God. That is precisely what "Messiah" means: "anointed one."

In the Old Testament, which prophesies the coming of Christ, the term "anoint" is translated from Hebrew *mashah*. To anoint is to consecrate one's future stead by means of the application of a mark; usually oil. In its root form, *mashah* means "to smear." As such, anointing is a sign. It is not the application of a magic potion, but the mark of one who has been previously called by God to a task. Kings were anointed by prophets at God's direction. Such did not empower them to be king; they were empowered by God's sovereign call. "Christ," "messiah" and "anoint" all have the same meaning; the consecrated One who was chosen in advance by God. Yet, anointing is merely the mark of such a call- not its source of power. When Dollar asks, "why did God have to anoint him," he asks a circular and ridiculous question. Christ was anointed by merit of who he was; he was the One prophesied who would rule on David's throne, vicariously pay for the sins of man and fulfill the legal requirements of God's law to completion. He wasn't the Son of God

---

[66] 1 Samuel 16:13

Chapter 9 - Atonement Heresy: Kenoticism

because he was anointed; he was anointed because he was the Son of God.

Dollar reveals his mistaken understanding of anointing even more thoroughly in his assertion that Jesus would show what "a man with the anointing" could do. Dollar seems to think that some superficial act of "anointing" gave Christ the ability to fulfill his office which he would not otherwise have had. In principle, Dollar is claiming that anointing gave Christ his power. The scriptures declare that Christ was pre-incarnate God. There is no oil that can empower the sovereign of all creation to a higher stead. This understanding is simply nonsense.

Yet, such understanding is a base of operation in the WoF movement. Anointing is understood as the impartation of a special gift rather than the identification of one who is thus gifted. The idea of Jesus being no different from other "anointed" men is nothing short of the idolatry of man. Such foolishness is precisely what would draw Copeland to make this outlandish claim:

> "The Spirit of God spoke to me and He said... a twice-born man whipped Satan in his own domain." And I threw my Bible down... like that. I said, "What?" He said, "A born-again man defeated Satan, the firstborn of many brethren defeated him." He said, "You are the very image, the very copy of that one."[67]

We will deal with Christ as a "born again man" in chapter eleven. But, Copeland, like Dollar, clearly understands Christ to be relegated to a mere human status without deity. Copeland believes (from his self-professed "word

---

[67] **Kenneth Copeland** *Substitution and Identification* audio, tape #00-0202, side 2)

from the Lord") that Jesus was equipped with no more power than Copeland himself, as a man who is "the very copy of that one (Christ)."

The very heart of WoF theology requires man to be capable of divine acts outside of God's intervention and enablement. After all, they assume that God used the same "force of faith" to create the world that man should use to fulfill his own needs. They presume that Jesus was no exception. He was a man of the same essence as Copeland himself, who defeated Satan from within the limitations of human abilities.

Traditional kenoticism draws its base of understanding from a flawed attempt at the exegesis of Philippians 2. That text notes,

> ***Philippians 2:5-8 (ESV)***
> *[5] Have this mind among yourselves, which is yours in Christ Jesus,*
> *[6] who, though he was in the form of God, did not count equality with God a thing to be grasped,*
> *[7] but made himself nothing, taking the form of a servant, being born in the likeness of men.*
> *[8] And being found in human form, he humbled himself by becoming obedient to the point of death, even death on a cross.*

The namesake of kenoticism is derived from the Greek term *kenoo (ken-ah'-o)*, which is translated "made himself nothing" in the ESV above. *Kenoo* literally means "to make void" or figuratively "to make of no reputation (as the KJV does translate it)," such as a king dressing in civilian clothes and walking the streets at night. Such is what this text states. "Jesus was God" but "took the form of a servant" by being "born in the likeness of men." This text affirms Jesus' divinity and his humanity. Clearly *kenoo*, in context, demonstrates God who becomes man without denigrating his nature as God. Jesus' emptying of himself was not a dismissal of his divine attributes, but rather a making of no consequence of them. As the reformers rightly noted, Christ yielded up "the independent exercise" of his divine attributes when he came as a man. Christ came as God entirely, yet lived as a man without God's reputation and glory. Such is the substance of the reference in verse 8, "And, being found *in human form*, he humbled himself...." To claim that Christ emptied himself of Godhood is to take excessive license with this text and to completely ignore the remainder of biblical testimony concerning Christ's nature.

Such other testimony from the same author, Paul, says of Christ in Colossians,

> *Colossians 2:9 (ESV)*
> *⁹ For in him the whole fullness of deity dwells bodily,*

Paul asserts the historic doctrine of Christ's nature: that he existed as fully God while in human flesh. If Christ had set his deity aside, how could he – bodily – have in him the "whole fullness of deity?" Even in traditional kenotic doctrine, which asserts that Christ put aside *part* of his divinity, he could not exhibit "the whole fullness" of deity in such a condition. Christ was fully God and fully human.

The false idea of *kenoo* indicating a Christ who had released himself from deity has failed muster in nearly all venues of traditional theology. It apparently lives on in the WoF movement, not because of Philippians 2, however, but due to Copeland's fireside chat with God about "things I never told the apostle Paul."

At the end of the day, the Jesus of the WoF doctrine is pre-existent God, who laid the entirety of his deity aside to come to earth as a completely normal human man such as you and I, but without a sin nature. This fits the corrupted WoF understanding of a "second Adam" in Christ. They claim that Christ came to earth as the second Adam, but in a completely human context.

For the record, the concept of a "second Adam" is a genuinely biblical proclamation - at least when one allows the Bible to reveal the metaphor in its own light. 1 Corinthians 15 notes,

> *1 Corinthians 15:42-49 (ESV)*
> [42] *So is it with the resurrection of the dead. What is sown is perishable; what is raised is imperishable.*
> [43] *It is sown in dishonor; it is raised in glory. It is sown in weakness; it is raised in power.*
> [44] *It is sown a natural body; it is raised a spiritual body. If there is a natural body, there is also a spiritual body.*
> [45] *Thus it is written, "The first man Adam became a living being"; the last Adam became a life-giving spirit.*
> [46] *But it is not the spiritual that is first but the natural, and then the spiritual.*
> [47] *The first man was from the earth, a man of dust; the second man is from heaven.*
> [48] *As was the man of dust, so also are those who are of the dust, and as is the man of heaven, so also are those who are of heaven.*
> [49] *Just as we have borne the image of the man of dust, we shall also bear the image of the man of heaven.*

The biblical imagery of a second Adam is clear from its context. The first Adam was "a living being" and the second "a life-giving spirit." This language follows the introductory concept of the nature of the resurrection of the dead: our bodies are "sown a natural body" and "raised a spiritual body." The metaphor, then, speaks to the first Adam as "natural body" and the second Adam,

Christ, who will raise us in his likeness with a "spiritual body."

This text specifically is dealing with the differences between a natural body and the coming spiritual body of all in Christ who will be resurrected from the dead. Such teaching highlights Christ's unique qualities as a second Adam. Christ is "the man of heaven" while Adam was "the man of dust." The metaphor of Christ as a second Adam thus serves to highlight Christ's divinity – not his humanity. Suffice it to say, biblical teachings concerning a second Adam are nothing like what it has been made into by WoF teachers.

WoF teachers have a God-complex concerning Adam. Their belief is that he was created as an equal with God and had the same fullness of God in the bodily form as Christ himself has. Ironically, they claim that Christ came to earth as a mere man while claiming that Adam was an exact duplicate of God. As such, their claims indicate that Adam was *superior* to Christ! He (Adam) was a duplicate of God himself, while Christ was merely human without deity. Dollar and Copeland maintain,

> "When God made Adam all He did was make an exact imprint of Himself. He duplicated Himself"[68]
> "Adam was God manifested in the flesh."[69]

Adding to the strangeness of this doctrine, Copeland further asserts that,

---

[68] **Creflo Dollar** *Our equality with God Through Righteousness*, January 21, 2001

[69] **Kenneth Copeland** - (Following the Faith of Abraham, Tape #01-3001)

Apostasy! | 105

> "Adam was made in the image of God. He was as much female as he was male. He was exactly like God. Then God separated him and removed the female part. Woman means 'man with the womb.' Eve had as much authority as Adam did as long as they stayed together."[70]

Aside from hints of Copeland's Oedipus complex, the gist of the WoF atonement process is the reinvention of the Adamic being in Christ himself; a new man made without a sin nature who would redeem the nature of man – wholly as a man.

Make no mistake; a Christ lacking deity is not the Christ of the scriptures. Such is an invention of the WoF movement, injected into their doctrines in order to convince their followers that they can be everything Jesus was – even to the point of being elevated to a "little god."

The scriptures articulate a completely contrary truth. Christ was fully God in human flesh. John claims,

> ***John 1:14 (ESV)***
> *[14] And the Word became flesh and dwelt among us, and we have seen his glory, glory as of the only Son from the Father, full of grace and truth.*

Christ's glory was the glory of the Son from the Father, "full of grace and truth," not the glory of an elevated man. Verse 10 notes,

> ***John 1:10 (ESV)***
> *[10] He was in the world, and the world was made through him, yet the world did not know him.*

He who made the world was in the world. He was not partially in the world, nor was only a human nature of

---

[70] **Kenneth Copeland** *Sensitivity of Heart* (Fort Worth: Kenneth Copeland Publications, 1984) 23

Christ in the world. The Christ who made the world was in the world.

Isaiah notes of the Christ,

> **Isaiah 9:6 (ESV)**
> *⁶ ... his name shall be called Wonderful Counselor, Mighty God, Everlasting Father, Prince of Peace.*

Paul maintains,

> **Colossians 2:9 (ESV)**
> *⁹ For in him the whole fullness of deity dwells bodily,*

It is not a partial fullness of Christ that dwelt bodily, but the whole fullness of deity which dwelt in Him. Such is the essential doctrine of Christ by which the church was built. To present that Christ was not God – even for a moment – is the epitome of misunderstanding the nature of who God is. One who is all powerful cannot become less. Nor can one who is not God become God by some mystical means of elevation. Such a notion demeans the very essence of what God is: eternally omnipotent, omniscient and omnipresent.

Jesus is, was and always has been fully God. In his advent, he was God in the flesh. If such were not so, biblical proclamations concerning atonement – that God is the justifier for sin – are built upon a failed premise. For, if Jesus were not fully God, then justification came from man, not God. Sadly, the next few chapters will reveal that such an inference is precisely what WoF teachers intend to present.

Chapter 10 - Atonement Heresy: Jesus in Hell

The WoF adventures in misunderstanding the nature of Christ, believe it or not, actually get much worse the further one investigates. It is apparently not sufficient to demote God to being at man's mercy and denigrate Christ as less than God while on the earth. Woefully, these teachers diminish Christ's nature even further by depreciating him to the point of becoming *satanic* through his suffering on the cross.

One of the most disturbing teachings of the movement revealed as of yet, WoF proponents actually contend that Jesus took the nature of Satan upon himself in order to secure the salvation of mankind. As their story goes, Jesus, when he died, ceased to be the son of God, went to Hell and literally became Satanic in order to punish sin.

Copeland asserts Jesus' descent rhetorically,

> "How did Jesus then on the cross say, 'My God.' Because God was not His Father any more. He took upon Himself the nature of Satan."[71]

According to this doctrinal deformity, "becoming sin for us" translates to Jesus literally becoming a satanic being, taking "upon Himself the nature of Satan."

Hinn concedes an equivalent sentiment as he notes,

---

[71] **Kenneth Copeland** (Believer's Voice of Victory, TBN, April 21, 1991)

> "He [Jesus] who is righteous by choice said, 'The only way I can stop sin is by me becoming it. I can't just stop it by letting it touch me; I and it must become one.' Hear this! He who is the nature of God became the nature of Satan where he became sin!"[72]

In the WoF understanding of atonement, Jesus literally took Satan's nature upon himself; that is to say that he became a satanic being, so that that he may properly be able to atone for the sins of man.

Hinn's phrase "became sin" comes from the misapplication of Paul saying,

> *2 Corinthians 5:21 (ESV)*
> *[21] For our sake he made him to be sin who knew no sin, so that in him we might become the righteousness of God.*

This text certainly illustrates Jesus' "becoming sin" for us through his death on the cross. While it says nothing whatsoever about a satanic nature, the text clearly maintains that he who knew no sin was caused "to be sin" on our behalf. The question that needs to be addressed is, does "to be sin" parallel with the idea of Jesus taking upon himself "the nature of Satan?"

The answer is a resounding, "no!" It does not mean that in the wildest translational variance. Jesus did not take on Satan's nature, nor did he become sinful, but rather, he became the object of God's wrath for *our* sin. In fact, the very idea that a supposed theologian would come up with such a nonsensical interpretation of this text reveals either that he is utterly ill-equipped to be teaching or that he has

---

[72] **Benny Hinn** (Trinity Broadcasting Network (TBN) 1 December 1990)

an external motive for intentionally misrepresenting the text; or possibly both. Even a cursory understanding of biblical atonement would prevent one from making such an adolescent error. The idea of Christ being without sin, yet being made "to be sin" comes from the Old Testament portrait of substitutionary atonement, which Christ fulfilled through his death on the cross.

The Greek term translated "to be sin" is the term *hamartia*. *Hamartia*, itself, literally translates "sin." The "to be" is added in some translations to help assimilate the idea into an English text. In some translations, words which are added into a text to help one understand the meaning are italicized. One will notice such italics in the NASB and KJV of this text for the words "to be." In the Greek, the phrase would directly be translated "him not knowing sin, on behalf of us, he (God) made sin." The picture has nothing to do with Jesus taking upon himself the nature of Satan. The "nature of Satan" attribute is a completely extra-biblical idea in atonement, created perhaps by the "revelation knowledge" of the WoF teachers, but certainly not from scripture. Scripture teaches widely concerning a sin nature, but never of Christ having a sin nature, nor certainly a satanic nature.

The term, *hamartia*, is translated "sin" 172 out of 174 uses in the New Testament. The understanding from the text is clearly that "he who knew no sin" was made "sin" for us- the recipients of his atoning work.

In the Old Testament, the idea of "becoming sin" is attributed to the work of the sin offering, or the sacrificial animal whose blood wrought atonement by its sacrifice. The Hebrew terms *chattath* or *chattaah* are used interchangeably to denote "sin" or the "sin offering" in Old Testament texts, depending on the context of their usage.

Chapter 10 - Atonement Heresy: Jesus in Hell

Adam Clarke states,

> The words חטאת *chattath*, and חטאת *chattaah*, frequently signify sin; but I have observed more than a hundred places in the Old Testament where they are used for sin-offering, and translated ἁμαρτια [hamartia] by the Septuagint, which is the term the apostle uses, 2 Corinthians 5:21: He hath made him to be sin (ἁμαρτιαν, A SIN-OFFERING) for us, who knew no sin.
> -- Adam Clarke's Commentary, Gen. 4:7 [bold transliteration added]

Thus, the idea of "becoming sin" is tantamount to saying that Christ became "the sin offering" required in the Old Testament Law. Indeed, Christ fulfilled the law as he predicted he would do.

> **Matthew 5:17 (ESV)**
> *17 "Do not think that I have come to abolish the Law or the Prophets; I have not come to abolish them but to fulfill them.*

Jesus "becoming sin" is the same idea as the atoning blood of the sacrificial goat on the Day of Atonement "becoming sin." He was the blood offered which paid the demands for God's justice against sin; *for the wages of sin is death,* and *the day you eat of it you will surely die.*[73] Sin has always born the penalty of death. God's grace provided the substitutionary atonement system, beginning with the old testament animal sacrifices, which pointed toward and were fulfilled by the final sacrifice of Christ himself; the provision of blood for the atonement of man's sin.

---

[73] Romans 6:23, Genesis 2:17

Apostasy! | 111

With a proper understanding of Old Testament atonement doctrine, it is unthinkable that a serious theologian would suggest that Christ's atoning work was tantamount to his "taking the nature of Satan" rather than the systematic fulfilling of his work of vicarious atonement by becoming a sacrifice on man's behalf. Yet, in the disingenuous system of WoF doctrine, this is precisely the assertion. Copeland concurs,

> "The righteousness of God was made to be sin. He accepted the sin nature of Satan in His own spirit. And at the moment that He did so, He cried, 'My God, My God, why hast thou forsaken me?' You don't know what happened at the cross. Why do you think Moses, upon instruction of God, raised the serpent upon that pole instead of a lamb? That used to bug me. I said, 'Why in the world would you want to put a snake up there; the sign of Satan? Why didn't you put a lamb on that pole?' And the Lord said, 'Because it was a sign of Satan that was hanging on the cross.' He said, 'I accepted, in my own spirit, spiritual death; and the light was turned off.'"[74]

Absolutely no biblical text teaches, infers or even hints that the eternal son of God took on the fallen and corrupt nature of Satan through his redemptive work on the cross. Such is tantamount to blasphemy; for it is calling the glorious and undefiled Son of God none other than Satan himself. The scriptures teach that is was Christ's *righteousness* that made him a suitable sacrifice for sin, not a satanic nature. And, the application of his righteousness to sin does not take away his righteousness – it takes away man's sin! Sin does not defeat Christ –

---

[74] **Kenneth Copeland** (What Happened from the Cross to the Throne, 1990, audiotape #02-0017, side 2)

Chapter 10 - Atonement Heresy: Jesus in Hell

Christ defeats sin by paying its penalty *by his righteous and substitutionary death.*

In Isaiah, God calls Christ "my righteous servant."

> ***Isaiah 53:11 (ESV)***
> *¹¹ Out of the anguish of his soul he shall see and be satisfied; by his knowledge shall the righteous one, my servant, make many to be accounted righteous, and he shall bear their iniquities.*

God's righteous servant, Christ, bears the iniquities of sinful man. He is a substitution; righteousness given on behalf of the unrighteous, bearing their sins, though he was without sin himself. Jesus' "becoming sin" referred to his paying the guilt of the sins of others, *not* his becoming satanic. Isaiah continues,

> ***Isaiah 53:12 (ESV)***
> *¹² Therefore I will divide him a portion with the many, and he shall divide the spoil with the strong, because he poured out his soul to death and was numbered with the transgressors; yet he bore the sin of many, and makes intercession for the transgressors.*

The WoF teaching that Jesus took the nature of Satan is egregiously deceptive, erroneous and quite deliberately misplaced; simply because it fits the WoF model and serves their purposes of exalting man (not to mention Satan) while demoting God.

It should further be noted that by "becoming satanic," the WoF movement is suggesting that Satan himself played a role in the salvation of mankind! If Christ had to take on Satan's nature, then Satan's nature was a required element of atonement.

Make no mistake: to equate the work of the Holy Spirit to the work of Satan is the substance of the unpardonable sin committed by first century Israel. Such is precisely the context of Matthew 12. Jesus healed a mute demoniac; something which the Jews understood that only Messiah could do. The people rightly asked the question, "Can this be the Son of David?"[75] They understood his work of healing a mute demoniac to be a messianic sign. In response, verse 24 notes,

> **Matthew 12:24 (ESV)**
> *²⁴ But when the Pharisees heard it, they said, "It is only by Beelzebul, the prince of demons, that this man casts out demons."*

The Pharisees, having seen Jesus' messianic miracle, attributed this work to Satan. It is this very attribution of the work of the Holy Spirit to the work of Satan of which Christ proclaimed the only unforgivable sin: blasphemy of the Holy Spirit. Jesus responded,

> **Matthew 12:27-31 (ESV)**
> *²⁷ And if I cast out demons by Beelzebul, by whom do your sons cast them out? Therefore they will be your judges.*
> *²⁸ But if it is by the Spirit of God that I cast out demons, then the kingdom of God has come upon you.*
> *²⁹ Or how can someone enter a strong man's house and plunder his goods, unless he first binds the strong man? Then indeed he may plunder his house.*
> *³⁰ Whoever is not with me is against me, and whoever does not gather with me scatters.*
> *³¹ Therefore I tell you, every sin and blasphemy will be forgiven people, but the blasphemy against the Spirit will not be forgiven.*

It is essential that one understand the nature of the unpardonable sin: it was the attributing of the work of the Holy Spirit to Satan. This, Jesus said, "will not be forgiven."

---

[75] Matthew 12:23

Chapter 10 - Atonement Heresy: Jesus in Hell

When a WoF teacher claims that Christ – by taking upon himself the nature of Satan – was able to provide atonement for sins, are they not attributing the work of the Holy Spirit to Satan? Does such not present Satan as the agent of salvation rather than the Spirit of God?

But even at this point they do not stop condescending Christ and exalting Satan's role in atonement. They actually go so far as to teach that Christ suffered in Hell – *at the hand of Satan* – to pay for the sins of man!

Copeland, in his earlier quote, continues:

> "How did Jesus then on the cross say, 'My God?' Because God was not His Father any more. He took upon Himself the nature of Satan. And I'm telling you Jesus is in the middle of that pit. He's suffering all that there is to suffer, there is no suffering left . . . apart from him. His emaciated, little wormy spirit is down in the bottom of that thing and the devil thinks he's got him destroyed. But, all of a sudden God started talking."[76]

More quotes from WoF teachers will follow shortly, but make no mistake about the premise: WoF teachers proclaim that *Jesus was punished in Hell by the hand of Satan to pay for our sins.*

This theology is referenced by WoF teachers as being derived from Psalm 16 or, in some references, the Apostles Creed. One of the most misunderstood sentiments of the Apostles' Creed is the referral concerning Christ that, "He descended into hell." The conclusion of the Apostles' Creed is good and legitimate.

---

[76] **Kenneth Copeland** (Believer's Voice of Victory, TBN, April 21, 1991)

The failure which leads to the controversy is a misunderstanding of what the framers of the creed meant by their use of the term, "Hell."

"Hell" is an English term. It has no singular biblical Greek or Hebrew equivalent which describes it accurately according to its modern English usage. The English term references several differing Greek and Hebrew terms in various translations. Furthermore, translations tend to use the term within the cultural understanding of the generation to which the translation was written. Older translations use the term in a different way than newer translations use it.

The English term "Hell" comes from the Saxon "*helan*," which means "to cover" or "to hide." Hell, in its original English usage, referred to the unseen place of the dead. It did not speak of "the lake of fire" in its original usage, but rather generally of "the place of the dead." The Hebrew term *Sheol* and the Greek term *Hades* are the most legitimate terms for one to understand the meaning of Hell in its *original* historical usage; "the place of the dead."

Language, however, has a tendency to drift. Terms which mean one thing in one generation come to new meanings as time passes. The English term "gay" has certainly transformed its fundamental meaning over the years. A gay man was once considered happy. Today the same phrase would describe a homosexual to most all who hear it. Likewise a "mad" person was once considered to be mentally deranged rather than angry, as it is commonly understood today.

Hell, in its original usage meant simply "the place beyond the land of the living." It could equally refer to the righteous or the unrighteous, as both die and are relegated to the place of the dead. The King James Version, written

Chapter 10 - Atonement Heresy: Jesus in Hell

in 1611, speaks prophetically of Christ, in Psalm 16, using the original understanding of "hell" in its translation.

> **Psalm 16:10 (KJV)**
> *^{10} For thou wilt not leave my soul in hell; neither wilt thou suffer thine Holy One to see corruption.*

Truly, Psalm 16 speaks of the coming Christ. Truly, it states that he will not be left "in Hell," in the King James Version. However, one's understanding of what exactly Hell is in 1611, when the KJV was published, is not the same as the common use of the term today, as most modern readers understand the term to refer instead to "the lake of fire," which is *not* what the Psalmist speaks of.

The underlying Hebrew word in Psalm 16:10, translated "Hell" by the King James Bible, is the term *Sheol*. *Sheol*, in the Old Testament is a place where *all of the dead of humanity* will rest until their appointed time. It is not synonymous with the lake of fire, or "Hell" as we know the English term today.

Sheol was a place where the righteous *and* the wicked went prior to the resurrection of Christ, at which point the righteous no longer went there, but directly to Heaven.

Hosea uses the same term (Sheol):

> **Hosea 13:14 (KJV)**
> *^{14} I will ransom them from the power of the grave; I will redeem them from death: O death, I will be thy plagues; O grave, I will be thy destruction: repentance shall be hid from mine eyes.*

Here, the KJV uses the term "grave" as an English translation of the very same Hebrew term, *Sheol*. And, clearly from this text, the Lord will "ransom" his *righteous* ones from *Sheol*. Indeed he did. When Christ died, he went where dead people went- to Sheol, or *Hades (in the Greek),* which is the same term rendered in the Greek New Testament. And, when Christ rose, he emptied the righteous out of Sheol/Hades and took them with him to Heaven, as noted in Ephesians:

> **Ephesians 4:7-9 (ESV)**
> [7] *But grace was given to each one of us according to the measure of Christ's gift.*
> [8] *Therefore it says, "When he ascended on high he led a host of captives, and he gave gifts to men."*
> [9] *(In saying, "He ascended," what does it mean but that he had also descended into the lower regions, the earth?*

The Apostles' Creed speaks of a pure and original understanding of the term Hell, which refers to the hidden place of the dead: Hades. Christ died, went to Hades, and rose from it, bringing with him all of those who waited for his victory over death. Likewise, when the King James Bible speaks of Jesus not being left *in Hell,* it is translating the term *Sheol,* the general place of the dead.

David wrote in Psalm 139 the following:

> **Psalm 139:8 (KJV)**
> [8] *If I ascend up into heaven, thou art there: if I make my bed in hell, behold, thou art there.*

Using the KJV, once again the term "Hell" is rendered for *Sheol.* The NIV, however renders the following:

> **Psalm 139:8 (NIV)**
> [8] *If I go up to the heavens, you are there; if I make my bed in the depths, you are there.*

Likewise, the ESV,

> **Psalm 139:8 (ESV)**
> [8] *If I ascend to heaven, you are there! If I make my bed in Sheol, you are there!*

The underlying term, *Sheol,* does not refer to an eternal lake of burning sulfur – or Hell by today's understanding of that term - but rather the unseen abode of the dead. Did David really consider himself prepared to make his bed in the eternal lake of fire at some future point? Perhaps soon the WoF teachers will have David paying for the sins of man in Hell. It's just as ridiculous of a thought as to think that Jesus went to the lake of fire which people commonly call "Hell" by today's language standards.

Modern versions account for the development of the cultural understanding of what the term "Hell" is understood to be, and use other terms so as not to cause modern readers, who believe Hell to be synonymous with the lake of fire, to misunderstand the text.

Most modern translations, such as the NASB, translate this text using the original Hebrew term to avoid misunderstandings:

> **Psalm 16:10 (NASB)**
> [10] *For You will not abandon my soul to Sheol; Nor will You allow Your Holy One to undergo decay.*

This lengthy explanation is essential to allow the reader to understand without question a simple fact: *Jesus did not go to the lake of fire,* where the eternal punishment for sins is realized. He went where dead people went; to Hades, because he died as a human, and followed the natural course of a dead man to that place. [For a more detailed explanation of the realms of the afterlife, see my book, *The Spirit World.*]

And, here begins the issue with the misuse of scripture in the hands of the WoF teachers. Simply stated, they teach that Jesus literally went to Hell - in the modern understanding of the term, *the lake of fire* - and that he suffered in Hell to pay the penalty of sin for mankind. Such is unmistakably the implication of Copeland's wholly misrepresented notion that Jesus suffered in Hell at the hands of Satan. But he continually makes that very assertion, noting,

> "In hell He [Jesus] suffered for you and for me. The Bible says hell was made for Satan and his angels. It was not made for men. Satan was holding the Son of God there illegally ... The trap was set for Satan and Jesus was the bait."[77]

For the record, the Bible does in fact state that the eternal lake of fire was made for Satan and his angels in Matthew 25:41. In that text the phrase "eternal fire prepared for the Devil and his angels" is used. Clearly, the eternal lake of fire *was prepared for the devil and his angels.* Jesus did not use the term Hades in this text, however. He was speaking of the lake of fire- not the abode of the dead prior to Revelation 20:14, at which point "death and Hades were thrown into the lake of fire." Hades is temporary – the lake of fire is the eternal abode of the unrighteous upon the Day of Judgment.

WoF teachers teach that Jesus went to Hell, using the modern definition of what Hell is. In short, they teach that Jesus went to the lake of fire, the place of torture and punishment, on behalf of man to pay the penalty of man's sin by being tortured in Hell.

The problem with this misapplication of scripture and misunderstanding of proper atonement theology is simple: if Jesus paid the price of man's sin in Hell, then what was

---

[77] **Kenneth Copeland** *Walking in the Realm of the Miraculous* (Kenneth Copeland Ministries, 1979) 77

Chapter 10 - Atonement Heresy: Jesus in Hell

he doing on the cross? Did his death on the cross serve any purpose, other than getting him dead?

Not according to these teachers. Their clear and repetitive claim is that Jesus' work on the cross accounted for virtually *nothing*. They teach that it was not Jesus' death which provided salvation for mankind, but his suffering in Hell. Copeland states that a physical death on the cross *was not what was required for salvation!* He notes,

> "Every prophet that walked the face of the earth under the Abrahamic covenant could have paid the price if it were a physical death only. When he said 'It is finished' on that cross, he was not speaking of the plan of redemption. The plan of redemption had just begun; there were still three days and three nights to be gone through."[78]

No prophet that walked the earth could have paid the price for sin, for all were guilty themselves! Such statements indicate an utter disdain for biblical doctrines. Yet, the flagrantly-false prophet, Joyce Meyer, also agrees.

> "He [Jesus] was pronounced guilty on the cross but he paid the price in Hell."[79]

According to WoF doctrine, the plan of redemption was utterly incomplete upon Jesus' death on the cross. It was not Jesus' death which bought atonement for man, but his suffering in Hell. Indeed, "every prophet that walked the

---

[78] **Kenneth Copeland** (What Happened from the Cross to the Throne, 1990, audiotape #02-0017, side 2)

[79] **Joyce Meyer** *What Happened from the Cross to the Throne* (audio (now unavailable))

face of the earth" could have "paid the price if it were a physical death only." If this were true, then one could factually assert that the Bible *does not contain* the plan of salvation; for the Bible never states that Jesus suffered in Hell at the hands of Satan.

Ever.

It is a complete fabrication from one of Copeland's intimate chats with whom he thinks was God.

In this manner of thinking, Jesus' death on the cross is utterly misunderstood by the whole of theological history. And, according to this libelous doctrine, God's word is erroneous when it states that God worked *"through him [Christ] to reconcile to himself all things, whether on earth or in heaven, making peace by the blood of his cross."* **Colossians 1:19-20 (ESV)**

Paul understood atonement to come "by the blood of his cross" rather than through some future suffering in Hell, of which Paul never speaks. Does the cross have any power at all to these people? Is it merely one of numerous instruments of death by which Jesus could gain passage to Hell, where the real work was done? Is the focus on the cross this past two thousand years mere foolishness? Perhaps it is to these who do not serve under its banner.

> *1 Corinthians 1:17-18 (ESV)*
> [17] *For Christ did not send me to baptize but to preach the gospel, and not with words of eloquent wisdom, lest the cross of Christ be emptied of its power.*
> [18] *For the word of the cross is folly to those who are perishing, but to us who are being saved it is the power of God.*

Clearly, the cross of Christ is the power of God to those who know him, but only foolishness to those who are perishing. Note clearly Paul's mission to preach the *true* gospel, "*lest the cross of Christ be emptied of its power.*" The true gospel *is a gospel of the cross of Christ.* It is not a mythological and unbiblical tale about demons overpowering their creator in the eternal abode of burning fire which was intended as their own punishment.

Yet, in the teachings of the Word of Faith movement, the cross has truly been emptied of its power. It is honestly non-essential in their opinion. Meyer notes,

> "And you've got to really glean some things out of the Word of God to really get hold of what he [Jesus] did for you during those three days. Jesus said, 'It is finished.' And he meant the Old Covenant. The job he had to do was just getting started. He really did the job the three days and nights that he was in hell. That's where the job was done."[80]

The cross of Christ is wholly without substance in a system where "the job was done" in Hell.

At this point, the silliness of the notion that Satan himself would punish Jesus in Hell should also be considered. This idea is utter foolishness for three reasons.

First, it is foolishness because Jesus did not go to Hell, or the lake of fire, but Hades (the Greek equivalent of Sheol) as has been noted.

Secondly, it is foolishness because Hell is not yet open for business. The modern understanding of Hell, which these teachers use in their argument, is called either *Gehenna* or *the lake of fire* in the New Testament. This final place of eternal destruction, according to scripture, is not yet

---

[80] **Joyce Meyer** *What Happened from the Cross to the Throne* (audio (now unavailable))

populated, but is empty, awaiting the final judgment of the unrighteous. The "ribbon cutting" for the lake of fire is demonstrated clearly in the Bible to be a future event.

First into the lake of fire are those judged upon Christ's return, as he noted in Matthew 25.

> **Matthew 25:41 (ESV)**
> [41] *"Then he will say to those on his left, 'Depart from me, you cursed, into the eternal fire prepared for the devil and his angels.*

Immediately following them into the eternal lake of fire are the beast and the false prophet.

> **Revelation 19:20 (ESV)**
> [20] *And the beast was captured, and with it the false prophet who in its presence had done the signs by which he deceived those who had received the mark of the beast and those who worshiped its image. These two were thrown alive into the lake of fire that burns with sulfur.*

They will be followed by Satan himself. (Read Revelation 20:1-9 for full context)

> **Revelation 20:10 (ESV)**
> [10] *and the devil who had deceived them was thrown into the lake of fire and sulfur where the beast and the false prophet were, and they will be tormented day and night forever and ever.*

Lastly, the unrighteous dead of history who remain in Hades (the righteous were removed from Hades at Jesus' resurrection) will enter after their judgment from the great white throne.

> **Revelation 20:11-15 (ESV)**
> [11] *Then I saw a great white throne and him who was seated on it. From his presence earth and sky fled away, and no place was found for them.*
> [12] *And I saw the dead, great and small, standing before*

Chapter 10 - Atonement Heresy: Jesus in Hell

> the throne, and books were opened. Then another book was opened, which is the book of life. And the dead were judged by what was written in the books, according to what they had done.
> ¹³ And the sea gave up the dead who were in it, Death and Hades gave up the dead who were in them, and they were judged, each one of them, according to what they had done.
> ¹⁴ Then Death and Hades were thrown into the lake of fire. This is the second death, the lake of fire.
> ¹⁵ And if anyone's name was not found written in the book of life, he was thrown into the lake of fire.

One will clearly note that "death and Hades were thrown into the lake of fire" at this future time. Though Satan will be in the lake of fire in this future time, he was *not* present at the time of Christ, and *is not* present currently in the lake of fire. His consignment into that abode is yet a future event. Thus, he could not possibly have been waiting in Hell for Jesus around 30 AD. The lake of fire was not yet opened for business.

Thirdly, the idea of Satan punishing Christ in Hell is foolish because it presumes that Satan has some sort of authority to punish his creator! He certainly has no authority to punish Christ, but neither does he have authority to punish any beings that are cast into Hell. This postulate comes from superstition, bad "Hell" jokes and wives tales. Satan is not the proprietor of Hell, but will be an inmate of Hell himself. Even Copeland seems to understand this, though his theological postulating skips over his own realization of this truth.

> The Bible says hell was made for Satan and his angels. It was not made for men. Satan was holding the Son of God there illegally ... The trap was set for Satan and

Jesus was the bait."[81]

Aside from Copeland's obsession with unbiblical mystical legalities, indeed eternal fire *was* created for the future punishment of Satan and his angels. But it was not created to be his front office, his operational center or his vacation home. The lake of fire is a place of *punishment* whereby Satan and his angels are to be destroyed for all eternity. How can one's intended place of eternal punishment somehow become *his personal* place of mastery over others? Did Satan go to Hell and take over his own prison? Only the most immature biblical student could rationally hold to such a claim.

It makes no logical sense whatsoever to presume that Hell is an abode where Satan would have authority to punish Christ. It is Christ who created Hell to punish Satan! And, God has authority over Hell, not Satan. *If* Christ were to go to Hell, and *if* Satan were to have been there to meet him, *even then* Satan would have no authority to punish Christ there. Hell belongs to Christ, and is a place where *God* punishes the wicked- *including* Satan. It is not Satan's personal play pen, but his own eternal prison of death.

These teachers are a mockery to the legitimate field of theological study. Their doctrines fail biblical muster at every turn. They are not remotely close to any logical, biblical or historic faith. They are aimlessly wandering in a theological wasteland of their own creation. I am convinced, however, that they are not stupid, but rather very intelligent. Their doctrinal illiteracy does not stem from their lack of capacity to study scripture properly, but from their very intentional resolve not to do so.

---

[81] **Kenneth Copeland** *Walking in the Realm of the Miraculous* (Kenneth Copeland Ministries, 1979) 77

Willingly, they twist scripture to meet their own needs, all the while leading millions into eternal destruction with them. Who will save these teachers in that day from having their eyes clawed out by their deceived followers for all eternity?

Chapter 11 – Atonement Heresy: Jesus' Salvation

With runaway revelation knowledge, a completely off-base understanding of faith, a demoted God, elevated man, non-deific Christ and Satan in charge of the punishment for man's sins one may wonder how this movement could possibly wander further from the truth. But rest assured that they can. These charlatans are not through with their systematic untying of the knot of valid theology. According to the WoF, there is still an issue remaining for Christ to be able to achieve the atonement for mankind: he, *Christ*, must be born again. You read it correctly: they teach that Christ, our Lord, because he had become satanic in nature, had to be born again to complete the purposes of his torture in Hell.

Copeland once again reveals to us that which could not otherwise have been known,

> "He [Christ] allowed the devil to drag Him into the depths of hell as if He were the most wicked sinner who ever lived ... Every demon in hell came down on Him to annihilate Him ... [They] tortured Him beyond anything that anybody has ever conceived ... In a thunder of spiritual force, the voice of God spoke to the death-whipped, broken, punished spirit of Jesus ... [in] the pit of destruction, and charged the spirit of Jesus with resurrection power! Suddenly His twisted, death-wracked spirit began to fill out and come back to life ... He was literally being reborn before the devil's very eyes. He began to flex His spiritual muscles

Chapter 11 – Atonement Heresy: Jesus' Salvation

> ... Jesus Christ dragged Satan up and down the halls of hell ... Jesus ... was raised up a born-again man ... The day I realized that a born-again man had defeated Satan, hell, and death, I got so excited ... !"[82]

Before scripturally mocking this unfathomable heresy, I must firmly establish an obvious but very important note about it. *There is not one biblical statement in this quote.* Not one. Literally every line quoted above from the hand of Ken Copeland came directly from the imagination of man. Never in scripture is a demon referenced as annihilating Jesus, Jesus' being tortured in Hell, his being punished by Satan for sin or his being "reborn before the devil's eyes." And some actually think I'm too hard on these teachers. Is that even possible? Have we forgotten how theology is formed? Has our post-modern world, with its lack of faith in *anything* robbed even the church of its *source* of true doctrine? Are we to contend along with the Starbucks generation that *whatever one thinks* is susceptible to validity simply because it is capable of being thought? That is not theology, friends, but is the root instead, of paganism. Theology, to the Christian, has *God as its source and the Scriptures as its testimony.* Understanding God's revelation to man through the verified biblical canon is the essence of the discipline.

The first step, then, in achieving valid theology is to identify the valid *source* of theology; that means by which God rendered revelation of himself to man. That source is scripture! *Sola scriptura* (by scripture alone) was a foundational principle of the reformation. It was because Christianity had become cultic, by adding human

---

[82] **Kenneth Copeland** ("The Price of it All," Believer's Voice of Victory, September 1991, p. 4)

Apostasy! | 129

inference and history into the "mix" of theological truth that the reformation was even necessary. The moment supposed "revelation knowledge" gets involved in the teaching of doctrine one is turning over the reins of their relationship with God to another lost, sinful and utterly incapable individual. It is the blind leading the blind in full living color. In this case, untold thousands are allowing Kenneth Copeland to literally re-write *the Bible* concerning the message of salvation, because Ken and the Bible clearly have very little to say in common regarding atonement in Christ. If there be any doubt as to my position, let me state it more clearly: Ken Copeland, and his Word of Faith followers *are not teaching* biblical theology, but cultism; defined as a teaching which adds to the truths of the Bible to define its source of revelation.

To trust Ken Copeland rather than one's Bible in matters of theology is tantamount to asking a four year old how to spell "onomatopoeia," while considering Webster's Collegiate Dictionary outdated on the subject. The Bible has remained unassailable for thousands of years. Historically speaking, Copeland and the WoF platform as a whole have just walked onto the playing field. He, nor any man alive should be granted the privilege of teaching theological truth outside of the standards of the Bible, the unchanging source of theological revelation to mankind. In the worldview of Christianity, one who does that should be considered a cult leader, just as Jim Jones, David Koresh and Sun Myung Moon were, *because they taught extra-biblical revelation.* I can't help but wonder; if David Koresh had a television show on TBN, would he have been accepted by today's church? Personally, I fear that he would.

That being said, allow me to demonstrate *biblical* soteriology rather than opinion in light of the WoF false doctrines. While every part of Copeland's above quote is false (other than perhaps Copeland being "excited") scripture teaches directly contrary to the foundational notions of it.

The idea of Satan punishing Christ has already been dealt with, as have the notions of Christ being sent to the abode of eternal punishment for the payment of sin. Yet, in the midst of this plethora of doctrinal error lies an assertion that is simply astounding: *Jesus had to be saved!*

The key issue with this claim is that it is built upon the assumption that Christ *needed* saving. Christ had no need of being saved because he was not sinful, not satanic and is in fact the very agent of salvation itself. The author of Hebrews notes,

> *Hebrews 9:14 (ESV)*
> [14] *how much more will the blood of Christ, who through the eternal Spirit offered himself without blemish to God, purify our conscience from dead works to serve the living God.*

Hebrews 9 notes in plain language that Jesus' offering of himself was one of purity. He "offered himself without blemish to God" which enables him to "purify our conscience from dead works to serve the living God." The idea of Jesus being "converted" to a sinner through the inventive and unbiblical "taking upon himself the nature of Satan" has no merit in the true and trustworthy account of atonement in scripture. Jesus never sinned. The *entire point* of a substitutionary atonement is that a pure and flawless blood sacrifice must be offered as a substitute for one's sin. Hebrews 9-10 paint a clear picture of Christ's having vicariously become the final act of substitutionary atonement in the vein of the Old Testament sacrificial system. Even in the Old Testament God rejected sacrifices offered by means of flawed and unworthy substitutions.

Apostasy! | 131

Malachi 1:8 (ESV)
⁸ When you offer blind animals in sacrifice, is that not evil? And when you offer those that are lame or sick, is that not evil? Present that to your governor; will he accept you or show you favor? says the LORD of hosts.

If God would not accept an unworthy animal sacrifice, it is inconceivable that he would accept a sinful human sacrifice via the transformed "satanic" Christ. The text of Hebrews further notes that the blood of Christ was offered without blemish. Copeland's assertion was that when God transferred the sins of the earth onto Christ at his death that he thus took on the nature of Satan. If that were true, then his blood would not be unblemished. But Christ *was* unblemished, sinless, perfect and acceptable to God even in his death. Jesus was the perfect sacrifice *precisely* because there was *no sin* in him, nor was there a sin nature or a Satanic nature. Christ "became" sin for us in a substitutionary fashion, taking the guilt of man's sin upon himself *specifically because he was pure and worthy to do so.* Substitution cannot be made by a satanic being,

1 Peter 1:19 (ESV)
¹⁹ but with the precious blood of Christ, like that of a lamb without blemish or spot.

Hebrews 4:15 (ESV)
¹⁵ For we do not have a high priest who is unable to sympathize with our weaknesses, but one who in every respect has been tempted as we are, yet without sin.

How, then, could Jesus be said to require a spiritual regeneration? How can one be born again when he has never sinned? I realize Copeland would suggest that Jesus required "saving" because he "took on the nature of Satan" on the cross. However, that assertion has been dealt with in this work already as a completely made up and unbiblical postulate; sadly, by men who know better.

Copeland further asserts in his delusion that Satan and the demons have *control over Christ* during this three day phantom visit to the lake of fire. He notes that, "Every demon in hell came down on Him to annihilate Him ... [They] tortured Him beyond anything that anybody has ever conceived."

It's almost comical that WoF teachers expect Jesus' followers to believe that he was subject to torture at the hand of demons. In case you haven't noticed, Ken, in biblical encounters between Jesus and demonic beings, it was the demons who cried out to *Jesus*, begging *him* not to torture *them!* They were petrified of Jesus' presence. Jesus was no rock star pastor from TBN; he was God incarnate, for crying out loud! Have you not read how demons responded to Christ in the scriptures?

> **Luke 4:33-34 (ESV)**
> ³³ *And in the synagogue there was a man who had the spirit of an unclean demon, and he cried out with a loud voice,*
> ³⁴ *"Ha! What have you to do with us, Jesus of Nazareth? Have you come to destroy us? I know who you are— the Holy One of God."*

Did *this* demon beat up Jesus? Interestingly, the text notes a single demon in this man. That single demon however asks the question, "Have you come to destroy us?" Speaking on his own behalf, and that of other demons not even present, this demon understands precisely what Jesus will do to them at a future point in time. He will destroy them all in the very lake of fire that Copeland assumes they use for weekend retreats.

In another text many demons, far outnumbering Christ, have a similar encounter. In this situation a man is overrun with demons.

Apostasy! | 133

> ***Mark 5:7-10 (ESV)***
> *⁷ And crying out with a loud voice, he said, "What have you to do with me, Jesus, Son of the Most High God? I adjure you by God, do not torment me."*
> *⁸ For he was saying to him, "Come out of the man, you unclean spirit!"*
> *⁹ And Jesus asked him, "What is your name?" He replied, "My name is Legion, for we are many."*
> *¹⁰ And he begged him earnestly not to send them out of the country.*

Even a group of demons, the spokesperson identifying himself as "legion" because of their numbers, *pleaded* with Jesus not to *torture them!* A legion in the New Testament is used to refer to a Roman regiment which, "in the time of Christ consisted of six thousand, exclusive of horsemen, who were in number a tenth of the footmen."[83] A vast group of demons, thus, feared torture at the hand of Christ, asking him not to harm them.

Copeland's hallucination of demons *torturing Jesus,* the almighty God incarnate, bears no resemblance to scriptural representations of demonic engagement with Christ. Demons feared Christ. They certainly did not engage him, for they knew their future estate, at his hands, was to be condemned and confined to the very eternal lake of fire which Copeland seems to think they were already occupying.

The apostle Paul also had a far different understanding of the relationship between the crucified Christ and the demonic kingdom. He notes that,

> ***Colossians 2:13-15 (ESV)***
> *¹³ And you, who were dead in your trespasses and the*

---

[83] Illustrated Bible Dictionary: And Treasury of Biblical History, Biography, Geography, Doctrine, and Literature.

> uncircumcision of your flesh, God made alive together with him, having forgiven us all our trespasses, ¹⁴ by canceling the record of debt that stood against us with its legal demands. This he set aside, nailing it to the cross.
> ¹⁵ He disarmed the rulers and authorities and put them to open shame, by triumphing over them in him.

According to Paul's testimony, Jesus disarmed the demonic rulers and authorities through his substitutionary death on the cross! Once again, Colossians demonstrates that Jesus' work was completed *by the cross,* rather than by Copeland's testimony of a mythical vacation to the lake of fire with the demons. And, the text demonstrates clearly that *victory over the demonic kingdom* was observed through Jesus' work *on the cross.* Thus, the risen Christ represented *even more* power to the demonic kingdom than the incarnate Christ, in whose presence the demons trembled.

Lastly, and perhaps most incredulous, is Copeland's assertion that Jesus Christ, the spotless unblemished Son of God, was "reborn" in Hell, as other men are reborn into spiritual regeneration. This simply defies logic, doctrine and the attitude of anyone who trusts in Christ as the once-for-all atonement for sins.

Copeland's confession was that Christ

> ...was literally being reborn before the devil's very eyes. He began to flex his spiritual muscles ... Jesus Christ dragged Satan up and down the halls of Hell ... Jesus ... was raised up a born-again man....

One might presume that if indeed a "born again" man is capable of paying the price of sin and providing salvation for others, then Christ is not unique in his status as our atoning sacrifice. If one can simply be "born again" and

Apostasy! | 135

therefore be worthy of being the sacrifice for sins, then perhaps anyone else could have been man's redeemer? One may hope that Copeland would never make such an outlandish assertion, or that I am taking liberties with his position. But, alas, I am not, for Copeland *does* make that very assertion.

> "The Spirit of God spoke to me and he said, "Son, realize this. Now follow me in this and don't let your tradition trip you up." He said, "Think this way -- a twice-born man whipped Satan in his own domain." And I threw my Bible down... like that. I said, "What?" He said, "A born-again man defeated Satan, the firstborn of many brethren defeated him." He said, "You are the very image, the very copy of that one." I said, "Goodness, gracious sakes alive!" And I began to see what had gone on in there, and I said, "Well now you don't mean, you couldn't dare mean, that I could have done the same thing?" He said, "Oh yeah, if you'd had the knowledge of the Word of God that he did, you could have done the same thing, 'cause you're a reborn man too."[84]

In Copeland's mind and solely in that imaginary realm I should add, Jesus' provision of salvation could have been granted by any born again man who "had the knowledge of the Word of God" that Christ had. In short, if you're theologically "smart" enough, *you* could be born again and counted as worthy to die for the sins of the world. This assertion, of course, relegates the entirety of Old Testament messianic prophecy null and void. The Old Testament prophecies, from Genesis to Malachi, understood a unique Messiah – chosen one, or anointed

---

[84] **Kenneth Copeland** (Substitution and Identification, tape #00-0202, side 2)

one – who *was God* to have been assigned by the Lord for the fulfillment of the law unto salvation. Never is there a hint that *anyone else* might be able to step into Messiah's stead. In fact, to even suggest such a wild allegation is excessively offensive to the gospel of Christ, which stands on the uncompromised premise – from Genesis to Revelation – that Christ, and *Christ alone* is the One by whom men must be saved. Christ did not "win" that position by a life well lived; he was the One assigned to that position by merit of his being the Son of God.

Peter unswervingly asserted,

> *Acts 4:11-12 (ESV)*
> [11] *This Jesus is the stone that was rejected by you, the builders, which has become the cornerstone.*
> [12] *And there is salvation in no one else, for there is no other name under heaven given among men by which we must be saved."*

According to Peter - and the scriptural authority by which he is enshrined and quoted - the name for which men must be saved is that of Jesus Christ alone! He is *the* unique messiah. There is "*no other name*." Not Muhammad, Krishna, Buddha, Koresh or Copeland. Copeland *could not* have died for your sins. The fact that he would even suggest as much indicates his arrogant disregard for the supremacy of Christ and his utter lack of affiliation with the God or the gospel of scripture.

It should also be noted, however, that Copeland's claim that God told him that he (Copeland) could have atoned for the sins of the world "'cause you're a reborn man, too" is completely circular. Copeland claims that any reborn man is capable to *purchase* the salvation of mankind if he has the knowledge of the Word of God that Christ had. This is a chicken and egg scenario. How can a reborn man purchase the salvation required to make him reborn? Either he was worthy or he was not. One cannot become saved in order to purchase the very same salvation. Whoever Copeland engaged in this enlightening conversation about circular rebirth, it was clearly not God.

God did not lumber onto the playing field of eternity when Copeland and the WoF gang first woke up to His existence. He had sovereignly prepared the advent of Christ from the very beginning, and the dawn of this coming King has *always had a unique personality*. In Genesis God states that *One* will come as the offspring of woman and bash the head of the serpent.[85] He told Abraham that a *unique seed* from his descendants would bless the entire earth.[86] He told Isaiah that this *One* would be afflicted for the sins of the world.[87] Psalm 2 calls him *"the Anointed One"* to utterly eliminate the possibility that His identity may be unknown in advance. Psalm 22 articulately describes his crucifixion and confession on the cross. In Luke, Mary was told she would have *a son* who would be called the "Son of God" whose kingdom will never end.[88] These prophecies did not align with Mohammad. They do *not* align in the person of Kenneth Copeland. There *is* no other name under heaven by which men must be saved but the name of Jesus Christ alone! Neither Krishna, Benny Hinn nor José Luis de Jesús Miranda in Houston, who claims to be Christ incarnate, have the privilege of being able to biblically assert that they "know the Word of God" well enough to provide salvation for man. That job, gratefully, has been taken. It

---

[85] Genesis 3:15

[86] Genesis 12:7

[87] Isaiah 53:5

[88] Luke 1:32-33

belongs to the unique Son of God incarnate; *one man*, pre-ordained from the beginning of time and revealed at a calculated point in history, to bring God's program of redemption to its climactic realization. I can think of no higher blasphemy than for Copeland, or anyone else, to claim they have the hypothetical potential to fulfill the advent of the promised Messiah who would be *pierced for their transgressions and crushed for their iniquities (Isaiah 53)*, if they only had sufficient enough knowledge of God's word.

WoF teachers continually and purposefully disregard, discredit and downright ignore scripture to advance their own agendas. Sadly, many who identify themselves with Christ shell out huge sums of money to keep them in practice. I can't emphasize enough how exceptionally important it is to note that Copeland is teaching a serious theological error for which *no biblical reference exists.* Copeland attempts to make it sound biblical, yet scripture comes far from catching his back. Supposed scriptural references for this bogus "truth" are absolutely comical; involving the complete reinvention of the Greek and English languages.

One text inadequately used to prop up Jesus' mythical spiritual rebirth is found in Colossians.

> **Colossians 1:18 (ESV)**
> [18] *And he is the head of the body, the church. He is the beginning, the firstborn from the dead, that in everything he might be preeminent.*

Colossians 1:18 notes that Christ is the *firstborn from the dead,* but speaks nothing of his being born again in the sense of a spiritual regeneration. *Firstborn* and *reborn* are not synonymous ideas in the least. While they sound similar enough for a good wordsmith to confuse and corrupt them, the terms themselves are completely different. The distinction of these two terms will be observed momentarily. Yet, this text fails to defend the "reborn" Christ assertion because it speaks of Jesus as the "firstborn" *from the dead*. Jesus is being noted as the first to be raised from death to life in eternal permanence. Others were resurrected from the dead temporarily, such as Lazarus, but each also died again. They were not raised to eternal life, but back to a normal, dying human existence. Christ, in the text, is noted to be the firstborn from among the dead to be raised to a *regenerated body*, which is eternal and cannot die, as noted in 1 Corinthians:

> ***1 Corinthians 15:50-53 (ESV)***
> *⁵⁰ I tell you this, brothers: flesh and blood cannot inherit the kingdom of God, nor does the perishable inherit the imperishable.*
> *⁵¹ Behold! I tell you a mystery. We shall not all sleep, but we shall all be changed,*
> *⁵² in a moment, in the twinkling of an eye, at the last trumpet. For the trumpet will sound, and the dead will be raised imperishable, and we shall be changed.*
> *⁵³ For this perishable body must put on the imperishable, and this mortal body must put on immortality.*

Jesus, being born of a natural human body, received upon his resurrection a glorified body - an imperishable body- which is fitting for life in Heaven. This is the promise, through Christ's work, to all who are redeemed. Thus, Jesus was the firstborn from among the dead in that he was the first to be born from the perishable earthly body to the eternal imperishable body of life. Jesus was regenerated *physically*, being the firstborn from among the dead.

Yet nothing is hinted at in the text concerning a *born again* condition, which will be examined momentarily and defined as a *spiritual* condition. The text speaks uniquely of a raised literal body rather than a spiritual rebirth. One must have first sinned and died spiritually to be enabled to be born again, or regenerated spiritually.

Another failed attempt at making this doctrine sound biblical is demonstrated in this very quote of Copeland. He clearly is attempting to credit his "Jesus born again" theology to Romans 8, noting, "A born-again man defeated Satan, *the firstborn of many brethren* defeated him." He attempts to equate the "firstborn of many brethren" in Romans 8:29 with the idea of Christ being "born again."

What he actually does, is misquote a section of scripture, knowing it would sound familiar to his audience, and thus falsely attempt to give credibility to his claim. What the text actually states is,

> **Romans 8:29 (ESV)**
> [29] *For those whom he foreknew he also predestined to be conformed to the image of his Son, in order that he might be the firstborn among many brothers.*

Copeland refers to Christ as the "firstborn among many brothers" in an attempt to describe Christ's phantom regeneration. Copeland attempts to associate "firstborn" with "reborn" as if the two terms are the same. But being "firstborn" is a completely different concept than is the idea of being "reborn." Many are firstborn in their families but are not reborn. Many are reborn but are not the firstborn. The biblical idea of the firstborn is the same as that concept in modern culture; the first who is born in a given family generation. Being reborn is not a physical concept, but a spiritual one. Rebirth, biblically, refers to spiritual regeneration through atonement. The two concepts are not even closely related. Yet, Copeland says Jesus was "born again…the firstborn of many brothers," in an attempt to make his doctrine sound biblical. It is not.

Apostasy! | 141

Nonetheless, in increasing measure teachers in the Word of Faith movement espouse this tragically erroneous teaching. Hinn has both feet on the same faulty platform, noting,

> "My, you know, whoosh! The Holy Ghost is just showing me some stuff. I'm getting dizzy! I'm telling you the truth--it's, it's just heavy right now on me....He's (referring to Jesus) in the underworld now. God isn't there, the Holy Ghost isn't there, and the Bible says He was begotten. Do you know what the word begotten means? It means reborn. Do you want another shocker? Have you been begotten? So was he. Don't let anyone deceive you. Jesus was reborn. You say, 'What are you talking about?' ...He was reborn. He had to be reborn. ...If He was not reborn, I would never be reborn. How can I face Jesus and say, 'Jesus you went through everything I've gone through, except the new birth?'"[89]

According to Hinn, even "begotten" means "reborn." Since when, one wonders?! Does *everything* mean "reborn" to these people?

There is exactly one Greek term which is translated in scripture as "begotten." That term is Greek, *gennao*, which means "be born," "bear" or to "be delivered." Begotten refers to physical birth; and therefore a *first* physical birth; for there is *but one* physical birth for anyone. Benny asks his ogling crowd "have you been begotten?" What a ridiculous question! *Everyone* has been begotten! It means, *to be born*, Benny! Birth happens to everyone!

---

[89] **Benny Hinn** - ("Our Position in Christ, Part 1", Orlando, FL: Orlando Christian Centre, 1991, videotape # TV-254)

"Reborn," which Benny claims to be synonymous with "begotten," does not appear in biblical Greek as a single term. "Reborn" in an English translation is also rendered "born again" in other translations. It is hopeful that Benny Hinn has never conducted a Greek study of this term, because "born again" (or "reborn" in some translations) comes from two Greek words, the first of which is *the exact same Greek term, gannao,* (born) yet is coupled with a second Greek term, *anothen,* which means, of course, "again," or "from above." "Begotten" is *gannao* and "born again" is *gannao anothen.* The two terms simply cannot be the same, as one term adds redundancy to the first with the idea "again" added to the picture. The first term invokes a singular action, while the other term denotes a secondary occurrence of action. To be born is to come out of one's mother's womb. To be born again is a *secondary* birth. In short, born does not mean born again in any sense, as the latter condition inherently implies that the former has occurred in a previous setting.

Another obvious problem with this assertion is failure to observe that being "born again" in scripture is a *symbolic* terminology. It refers to the state of spiritual regeneration by the use of symbolic language. This is why Nicodemus, in John 3, became confused when Jesus used the term "born again." To be born "again" makes no literal sense, because it is a symbolic term. That scenario details,

> *John 3:1-6 (ESV)*
> *¹ Now there was a man of the Pharisees named Nicodemus, a ruler of the Jews.*
> *² This man came to Jesus by night and said to him, "Rabbi, we know that you are a teacher come from God, for no one can do these signs that you do unless God is with him."*
> *³ Jesus answered him, "Truly, truly, I say to you, unless*

> *one is born again he cannot see the kingdom of God."*
> *⁴ Nicodemus said to him, "How can a man be born when he is old? Can he enter a second time into his mother's womb and be born?"*
> *⁵ Jesus answered, "Truly, truly, I say to you, unless one is born of water and the Spirit, he cannot enter the kingdom of God.*
> *⁶ That which is born of the flesh is flesh, and that which is born of the Spirit is spirit.*

Nicodemus, attempting to hear Jesus literally, does not know what to do with Jesus' statement "one is born again." He asks Jesus, "How can a man be born when he is old?" "Can he enter a second time into his mother's womb and be born?!"

Jesus clarifies the use of "born again" to Nicodemus as a metaphor for a *spiritual* condition. Being born again is explained by Jesus in that, "That which is born of the flesh is flesh, and that which is born of the Spirit is spirit." Thus, being "born" is a physical birth, but being "born again" is a spiritual birth as Jesus defined it.

This is why John 1 says,

> ***John 1:12-13 (ESV)***
> *¹² But to all who did receive him, who believed in his name, he gave the right to become children of God,*
> *¹³ who were born, not of blood nor of the will of the flesh nor of the will of man, but of God.*

According to John 1, secondary birth is spiritual in nature rather than physical. "Born" and "born again" have differing meanings even in their regular literal usage. However, in scripture, "born again" is *never* used in its regular, literal usage, but is *always* used metaphorically of a spiritual act. Being born again indicates one having been born "of God." It is the term symbolizing spiritual regeneration, while "born" is the term of physical birth.

Peter uses the same language.

Chapter 11 — Atonement Heresy: Jesus' Salvation

> **1 Peter 1:23 (ESV)**
> ²³ since you have been born again, not of perishable seed but of imperishable, through the living and abiding word of God;

Hinn's attempt to call Jesus "born again" simply because he was called "begotten" creates quite a difficult explanation on behalf of many who have been born. If "begotten" means "born again," then Hitler, Napoleon, Hussein, Bin Laden and the fish I ate for dinner last evening are all born again; because they all were "begotten."

Paul and Jan Crouch, the money behind the madness at TBN which coddles the antics of this movement, are always ready to lend a hand in the propagation of the unsound theses of their faithful workmen. Jan, quoting a book by Paul Billheimer, states,

> "[I]n order to be made alive unto God and restored to fellowship with His Father, He [Jesus] had to be reborn—for He had become the very essence of sin. Since sin had totally alienated Him from the Father, the only way He could be restored to fellowship with the Father was through a new birth to new life." [90]

The idea of Jesus being reborn is an important emphasis in this series of conjectures used to influence the pocketbooks of the collective WoF target audience. As God continues to be demoted, man is further exalted to the position where he can control his own destiny, provided he continues to support these duplicitous

---

[90] **Paul Billheimer** - (Destined for the Throne, special edition for TBN (Fort Washington, PA: Christian Literature Crusade, 1988 [orig. 1975]), 83-84. [**Quoted by Jan Crouch** - "Praise the Lord" television program, TBN (August 20, 1987)]

teachers who will demonstrate how this spiritual manipulation of God is supposed to function.

In the words of Paul,

> **Romans 16:17-18 (ESV)**
> [17] *I appeal to you, brothers, to watch out for those who cause divisions and create obstacles contrary to the doctrine that you have been taught; avoid them.*
> [18] *For such persons do not serve our Lord Christ, but their own appetites, and by smooth talk and flattery they deceive the hearts of the naive.*

Consider yourselves once again warned. It is imperative that you avoid, abandon and warn others of the teaching of these deceivers. By "smooth talk and flattery," such as telling you that you can be a "little god" – having the authority over the Word of Faith that God himself had – they deceive the minds of those who do not know better. None need to be naïve. We have the scriptures at our disposal that we may recognize the truth and avoid such error.

Chapter 12 - Healing in the Atonement

A seemingly benign and somewhat disconnected category of defective doctrines flowing from WoF sources is concerned with the nature of temporal health in the body of believers. Considering the group has consigned Jesus to a salvation in Hell, having an unbalanced view on physical healing seems almost orthodox. After all, there are a number of charismatic believers who come dangerously close to the teachings of the WoF on such subjects; while being utterly opposed to the WoF on others. Indeed most Christians believe God is capable of healing- and *does* in fact heal people of earthly ills. Yet, the WoF doctrine teaches that healing is a divine right of every believer in Christ; from the simple headache to heart disease, all are to be healed in the life of a Christian. In fact, the essence of the teaching is that a believer living rightly should never encounter sickness and disease at all. If one does, it is the fault of the believer himself, for God has granted the ability for each believer to be free from such physical limitations. Hinn illustrates,

> Sickness does not belong to you. It has no part in the Body of Christ. Sickness does not belong to any of us. The Bible declares if the Word of God is in our life, there will be health, there will be healing - divine health and divine healing. There will be no sickness for the saint of God. If Moses could live such a healthy life, so can you... He promises to heal all - every one, any, any whatsoever, everything - all our diseases!

> That means not even a headache, sinus problem, not even a toothache - nothing! No sickness should come your way.[91]

Hinn's famous "the Bible declares" is characteristically without a scriptural reference. I have scoured my own copies of scripture and can find no reference that even resembles "if the Word of God is in our life, there will be divine health." As has been noted, Hinn does not need a scriptural reference for his followers to agree. Yet, at times when one claims the scripture as an authoritative source it is common practice to *actually quote the text and reference;* something Hinn is exceptionally resistant to do.

WoF teachers however commonly claim the source of this doctrine from both poorly interpreted biblical references and/or the power of one's "word of faith" confessions in equal measure.

As to the scriptural evidence of their doctrines, the most proclaimed passage supposing to teach that healing belongs to every believer is found in Isaiah 53. Isaiah 53 is a Messianic prophecy and a favorite among prophetic chapters. It tells, for the first explicit time in the prophetic record, that Messiah would die for the sins of his people. In the context of that prophesied death Isaiah notes,

> *Isaiah 53:4-6 (ESV)*
> *[4] Surely he has borne our griefs and carried our sorrows; yet we esteemed him stricken, smitten by God, and afflicted.*
> *[5] But he was wounded for our transgressions; he was*

---

[91] **Benny Hinn** *Rise & Be Healed!* (Celebration Publishers, 1991) 14, 32

> *crushed for our iniquities; upon him was the chastisement that brought us peace, and with his stripes we are healed.*
> *⁶ All we like sheep have gone astray; we have turned—every one—to his own way; and the LORD has laid on him the iniquity of us all.*

Verse 4 notes, "He has borne our griefs" in the ESV. Other translations note "sicknesses" or "infirmities." Either term is a translation of the Hebrew word, *holî (kho-lee')*, which refers to sickness or calamity. Normally, by quoting either of these verses a WoF teacher asserts physical healing as a foundational element of the atonement of Christ. We *are healed*, they say, by the atoning work of Christ on the cross. Such a pronouncement requires some careful consideration.

There is no doubt that Isaiah 53 speaks of the coming Messiah, nor is it unclear that healing is fundamentally established as one of his works according to the text. In fact, Matthew notes,

> ***Matthew 8:16-17 (ESV)***
> *¹⁶ That evening they brought to him many who were oppressed by demons, and he cast out the spirits with a word and healed all who were sick.*
> *¹⁷ This was to fulfill what was spoken by the prophet Isaiah: "He took our illnesses and bore our diseases."*

Clearly Jesus had a healing ministry on earth which was depicted by verse 4, which describes Christ's life among the people in his earthly incarnation. The question that must be answered very carefully in this text, however, is *does the atonement of Christ guarantee the physical healing of every believer who follows him?* A simple reference to the earthly life of the Messiah and his healing ministry does not make such an assertion. Truly Christ healed untold numbers as Isaiah prophesied. But verse 4

Chapter 12 - Healing in the Atonement

does not equate such temporal healing of every believer as a guaranteed result of the atonement.

Biblical interpretation is not a cherry picking expedition. It is a slow, intensive and thoughtful process that requires, among other things, a right understanding of context. The overall context of Isaiah 53 as quoted above is that of the provision of atonement by Messiah through his substitutionary death. The prophet Isaiah writes very carefully in his text concerning the life of Christ and the death of Christ. It is exceptionally clear that the results of Messiah's sacrifice would be the atonement for sin.

It is the purpose and work of his atoning death which is in question concerning the healing of this chapter. The declaration of WoF teachers is not simply that "Jesus heals." Such would have certainly been a legitimate claim. Their doctrine teaches, rather, that *physical healing is a guaranteed result of the atonement for all Christians.* That is simply not what Isaiah 53 describes.

The term "healed" in verse 5 comes from a different Hebrew term, *rāpā' (ra-fah')*, which means to be healed in the sense of being mended or repaired. Surely "healing" is a fair translation of the term, but this term is also generally used to refer to healing of a figurative sort. In Genesis 20:17 God "heals" (*rapa*) Abimelech from his pending judgment. In Ezekiel 47:8 water was "healed" (*rapa*) from being undrinkable. In Jeremiah 19:11 pottery is referred to as never being "healed" (*rapa*) from being broken. The term, in short, has a meaning that far exceeds the simple understanding of diseases being treated. It is a more general term referring to the restoration or mending of its object. Such healing can be physical to a human life or an inanimate object. It is a restorative work, to be certain, but not necessarily a healing of sickness or physical defect.

Apostasy! | 151

Thus, the focal question to be addressed is, "what is being referred to as healed or restored by Christ's atoning work in verse 5?" The answer, of course, is found in the context of the passage.

If one had a conversation concerning a foot problem and noted that he had "been healed" by a certain product which was used, another would not for the reason of the statement "I've been healed" think that the person had unilaterally received healing from a cold which he may have had at the same time. The context of the discussion limits the scope of what was healed to the specific malady that was noted. The man in question is presumed healed from only the ailment which his circumstance referred.

Likewise, the context of Isaiah 53:5 and following note a healing or a mending of a *specific item* which resulted from the atoning work of Messiah: that singular item is **sin**. The result of Isaiah 53:5, stemming from the stripes inflicted upon Messiah, refers to a healing from the ailment of sin and is not automatically presumed to heal other ailments as its result. If that were not the case then we must assume that Messiah's suffering in Isaiah 53 were all about providing for the medicinal needs of man. While there is a guarantee of physical healing *in an eternal context*[92] granted in the atonement of Christ, temporal, earthly healing is not at all what Isaiah 53:5 is relating.

Isaiah makes four statements in verse 5 which amplify the *exact same subject matter.* Stated in verse 5 is a singular truth, using a Hebrew poetic device called *parallelism.* Parallelism, in this form, is a restating of a truth in two or more distinct manners as to enforce its understanding. Part one of the parallel notes that Jesus paid for our sins.

---

[92] Revelation 21:4

Chapter 12 - Healing in the Atonement

Part two of the parallel stipulates that by his payment, we are free from the penalty of our sins, or "healed" from sin's eternal consequences.

That Jesus paid for our sins is noted in the first phrase, "he was wounded for our transgressions." It is clarified in the second phrase, "he was crushed for our iniquities."

The nature of the freedom from sin purchased by his payment is noted in the third phrase, "upon him was the chastisement that brought us peace." And, that phrase is clarified in the fourth, "and with his stripes we are healed."

Simply put, the entire verse speaks on one unique truth: Messiah would die for our sins and by that death provide healing from *those sins*. The object of the healing is clearly defined in the first phrase, "he was wounded for *our transgressions.*" Transgressions, Hebrew *pasha*, refer to sin, rebellion and spiritual trespass. It is a very common term and is never defined as a physical defect, but a spiritual one. As such, the context of Isaiah 53:5 is that of a spiritual healing rather than a physical one.

The *entire context* of this passage relates to sin and Messiah's coming atonement for it. Other than the use of the term "healed," there is nothing in the text which would make one consider sickness to be an element of what Jesus was to do for mankind through the atonement noted in verse 5. This usage of the term "healed" does not merely refer to sickness. One can be healed from a broken bone. One can be healed from oppression. Likewise, one can be healed *spiritually,* from sin, as Isaiah 53:5 speaks of.

Verse 6 confirms sin as the object of this healing as it notes,

Apostasy! | 153

> *Isaiah 53:6 (ESV)*
> *⁶ All we like sheep have gone astray; we have turned—every one—to his own way; and the LORD has laid on him the iniquity of us all.*

Isaiah 53 tells one dynamic story from beginning to end: Messiah would come and pay the penalty of man's sin. Surely he invoked a healing ministry as part of the demonstration of his authority to Israel. Surely he had – and has – the power to physically heal whomever he so chooses. But the text never asserts healing from physical infirmities as a granted provision of his atoning death. What is guaranteed to be healed is the calamity of sin, by Messiah's vicarious offering of the penalty of sin; his death. Verse 12 concludes the matter,

> *Isaiah 53:12 (ESV)*
> *¹² Therefore I will divide him a portion with the many, and he shall divide the spoil with the strong, because he poured out his soul to death and was numbered with the transgressors; yet he bore the sin of many, and makes intercession for the transgressors.*

Jesus "bore the sin" of the world and made "intercession" for transgressors. Sin would be healed. The referenced healing of the atonement was thus spiritual in nature, not physical. The penalty for sin has been death from the very beginning. God did not say to Adam and Eve "the day you eat of it you will surely get sick," but "the day you eat of it you will surely die." If the "healing" provided by Christ's atoning sacrifice were to be understood as physical in nature, one would expect that men would stop experiencing physical death at all! But they do not- because Isaiah 53 speaks of the healing of man's *spiritual* condition as a result of Christ's atonement. He is healed *from sin,* being given a substitutionary atonement through the stripes of Christ's vicarious suffering.

Jesus heals. Of that there should be no biblical issue. Matthew confirms a healing ministry to have been referenced in Isaiah as a testimony to the person of Messiah. But healing is simply not a guarantee to every believer because of Christ's atoning work in Isaiah 53. I will always pray to Him for healing when in need. I will always have faith that *he can heal* if he so chooses. But it is a misinterpretation of the overall emphasis of Isaiah 53 to assert that healing – in this physical lifetime - is a guaranteed virtue of one's salvation.

Yet, according to WoF teachers, it is physical healing which Isaiah 53 uniquely speaks, and that healing is inherently available to all believers through the suffering of Christ on the cross. If you are a believer, then you have healing as a birthright in Christ.

Parsley notes,

> Healing is not a promise, healing is an established fact. Isaiah 53:5 shouts it, 1 Peter 2:24 resounds it and resonates it"[93]

Parsley at least has the resources to have noted that Peter quotes Isaiah 53:5, but he fails miserably at noting the context of either passage, as both are concerned with sin, not physical defect. What 1 Peter 2:24 "resonates" is that,

> **1 Peter 2:24 (ESV)**
> *²⁴ He himself bore our sins in his body on the tree, that we might die to sin and live to righteousness. By his wounds you have been healed.*

It is certainly accurate that 1 Peter "resounds...and resonates" Isaiah 53:5. But Peter's quoting of the text

---

[93] **Rod Parsley** (TBN Praise the Lord 12/04/2006)

illuminates healing from *sin* rather than physical ailments. Peter continues,

> *1 Peter 2:25 (ESV)*
> ^{25} *For you were straying like sheep, but have now returned to the Shepherd and Overseer of your souls.*

The redeemed were not like sheep because sheep are diseased or crippled, but because they *"were straying...but have now returned to the Shepherd and Overseer"* of their souls. Christ's atonement was concerned with the remedying of man's greatest ailment of sin. It was not the means by which Christians are guaranteed to avoid the flu, regain sight and/or experience relief from the temporal results of a fallen world. While Christ can and may heal temporal woes, such is not a pledged result of the atonement.

Promises of physical healing represent fundamentally useful pledges for the WoF emcee. Such insinuations draw prospective WoF converts into multi-million dollar facilities for their carrots. Such promises woo the extraction of the limited resources of countless disabled and ailing people into the coffers of WoF preachers. Simply put, healing sells in this marketplace. People want it, they will pay for it, and it is therefore promised by WoF teachers. Parsley, a proficient artist in this tactic, notes,

> "Salvation and healing are two gifts wrapped up in the same package. For God, healing is just as important and necessary as Salvation."[94]

The "package" Parsley speaks of is that of atonement. He believes that the blood which brought spiritual restoration

---

[94] **Rod Parsley** *The Backside Of Calvary* (Columbus: Results Publishing, 1991) 55

Chapter 12 - Healing in the Atonement

to mankind also brought healing to the bodies of believers in this lifetime. How ironic that Christ would say,

> **Matthew 18:8 (ESV)**
> *8 ... if your hand or your foot causes you to sin, cut it off and throw it away. It is better for you to enter life crippled or lame than with two hands or two feet to be thrown into the eternal fire.*

It does not sound as if Christ thinks "healing is just as important and necessary as salvation." Once again, scriptures fail to support the WoF paradigm.

Hinn concedes likewise, noting,

> "The Bible declares that the work was done 2,000 years ago. God is not going to heal you now — he healed you 2,000 years ago."[95]

Yet again, Hinn's Bible seems to be without chapter and verse annotation. He simply declares that which the Bible says without question. The assertion seems to be that *everyone already knows this.*

It should be highlighted in light of this near miss that scripture does teach that all believers will receive a new, glorified body which will never get sick and die. But, the reception of that body is upon the believer's resurrection to eternal life, rather than upon one's justification in this life. Paul notes clearly that healing from the confines of the body of death is a post-resurrection reality.

> **1 Corinthians 15:50-53 (ESV)**
> *50 I tell you this, brothers: flesh and blood cannot inherit the kingdom of God, nor does the perishable inherit the imperishable.*

---

[95] **Benny Hinn** *Rise & Be Healed!* (Celebration Publishers, 1991) 44

> *⁵¹ Behold! I tell you a mystery. We shall not all sleep, but we shall all be changed,*
> *⁵² in a moment, in the twinkling of an eye, at the last trumpet. For the trumpet will sound, and the dead will be raised imperishable, and we shall be changed.*
> *⁵³ For this perishable body must put on the imperishable, and this mortal body must put on immortality.*

To that end, one can truthfully say that *eternal* healing is guaranteed in the atonement; but temporal restoration from the penalty of sin is not. In fact, true and complete physical healing is simply not possible while confined to this judged body of death. If such were possible in this lifetime, why would Paul put such emphasis on promises of a future restoration? Why would he simply not tell the Corinthians to "claim their healing" now? Clearly Paul was not a Word of Faith proponent.

According to Paul, mortality is the nature of the bodies in which we live. It is for that reason that *"this perishable body must put on the imperishable and this mortal body must put on immortality."* To that end, one must understand that the penalty of sin given at the Garden of Eden, *"the day you eat of it you will surely die,"* involves a temporal judgment which *will endure* until that time when one receives the immortal body. Sickness and death came together into existence in a package deal. Sickness and death are the judged state of this human body. Atonement is the cure for sin and includes the promise of a resurrected, glorified body that will be free from both sin and death. But such is a future hope; not a present gift to be claimed by adhering to the non-biblical ranting of a WoF teacher.

Scripture simply does not assert that atonement and temporal healing are one and the same. Every attempt by WoF leaders to demonstrate such is a complete

Chapter 12 - Healing in the Atonement

fabrication or an aggressive misrepresentation of a biblical principle. Sadly, scriptural authority is candidly unnecessary for a WoF teacher to proclaim universal healing; for in their doctrine, whatever one wants is already otherwise accessible by one's proclamation of one's word of faith.

The second way, then, the WoF dealer presumes for one to receive healing in this life, is to use one's inherent abilities via the force of faith to achieve such goals. If you don't have what you think you need, such as healing, according to the WoF teacher, you can simply speak your creation into existence! Marilyn Hickey notes,

> "Say to your body, 'You're whole, body! Why, you just function so beautifully and so well. Why, body, you never have any problems. You're a strong, healthy body.' Or speak to your leg, or speak to your foot, or speak to your neck, or speak to your back; and once you have spoken and believe that you have received, and don't go back on it. Speak to your wife, speak to your husband, speak to your circumstances; and speak faith to them to create in them and God will create what you are speaking."[96]

Hickey uses the same formula for health that she claims for wealth, which will be examined in the next chapter. If you lack wealth, you speak to your wallet! If you lack healing, according to Hickey, you simply "speak to your body." A cursory online search will reveal literally hundreds of testimonies of people who have been duped into trying such foolishness. They come to a WoF pep rally, hear a rousing band followed by a false teacher, pay through the nose at the offering plate and leave with the

---

[96] **Marilyn Hickey** (Claim Your Miracles audiotape, #186, side 2)

Apostasy! | 159

very same affliction they "spoke to" for the past two hours. Sadly, these stories never make it past the editing room floor of the televised broadcast. These unhealed victims of religious larceny must resort to their own unfunded resources to tell their side of the story while the false teacher flies off in a private $6 million jet to the next fleecing.

Incongruously, such teaching not only continues, but grows persistently in popularity to those who so desire this healing message to be true. The word of faith missive promotes all of the luxury, health, wealth and happiness one can muster breath to confess.

One's simple profession of a faith-filled-word is expressly taught to bring the fruition of their heart's desire. Counter wise, WoF teachers propose the opposite formula as guaranteed failure. If one's word of faith is negative, then negative claims take shape by that spoken word. If one alleges to have a headache, the headache will never leave, prolonged by the very "word of faith" which claims it to exist. Price explains,

> "The believer should never die before the age of 70. That is the minimum and then they should live to be 120 years. This is done by faith words If you keep talking death, that is what you are going to have. If you keep talking sickness and disease, that is what you are going to have, because you are going to create the reality of them with your own mouth. That is a divine law."[97]

By "divine law" that exists on an undocumented page of Price's Bible, he contends that if one speaks of sickness

---

[97] **Frederick K.C. Price** *Living in the Realm of the Spirit* (Harrison House, 1989) 29

Chapter 12 - Healing in the Atonement

and disease, "that is what you are going to have, because you are going to create the reality of them with your own mouth." When all else fails, these teachers will go back to the rudiments of their theology and put the "word of faith" back in control of their circumstances; in spite of what scripture teaches on a subject. Whether healing, power or cold hard cash, the confession of one's mouth is the end-all source of funding according to this dogma.

Even America's child-like star pastor, Joel Osteen, has endorsed this bandwagon doctrinal farce. He clearly believes the same word- sovereignty notion, saying,

> "Start calling in divine health....You may have sickness in your body; you need to call in health. Words are like seeds; they have creative power."[98]

As is the premise of this work, bad doctrine leads to further bad doctrine. Suffice it to say, that once one has endorsed the root premise concerning the "word of faith," one can then control all outcomes, including the manipulation of one's own personal health. The end result demands that, if man has power of the word of faith, is a little god and God is no longer in control, then the full responsibility for health lies with the faith-word-confessing agent of man himself. All powers of life and death are in the hands of the speaker, as Copeland, Price and countless others assert.

> "As a believer, you have a right to make commands in the name of Jesus. Each time you stand on the Word, you are commanding God to a certain extent because

---

[98] **Joel Osteen** ("Speaking Faith Filled Words", Tape # 223, 2004)

it is His Word."⁹⁹

> "Yes! You are in control! So, if man has control, who no longer has it? God."¹⁰⁰

This leads to the most tragic of all possible doctrines regarding the physical healing of believers. For, according to the WoF teachers, the responsibility for one's healing, or lack thereof, is entirely upon themselves! If you are not healed, there is a problem with your faith and it is entirely *your own fault!* If one needs to merely speak in faith for something to happen, then clearly a failure of the experiment faults with the speaker's own lack of word-faith profession.

Continuing Hinn's earlier quote,

> "The Bible declares that the work was done 2,000 years ago. God is not going to heal you now — he healed you 2,000 years ago. All you have to do today is receive your healing by faith"¹⁰¹

It is thus it is *your job* to receive healing. If for some reason healing does not come, it must be your fault; for it was your job. Where has the notion of the sovereignty of God gone in this apostate faction? If such was ever understood at all its shelf-life has clearly expired. God's control over His universe is nowhere to be found in this human-centric doctrinal façade. Failure to receive lies purely on the professor. Anyone with an illness, injury or

---

[99] **Kenneth Copeland** *Our Covenant with God* (Fort Worth: Kenneth Copeland Publications, 1987) 32

[100] **Frederick K.C. Price** ("Prayer: Do You Know What Prayer Is ... and How to Pray?" The Word Study Bible, 1990 p. 1178)

[101] **Benny Hinn** *Rise & Be Healed!* (Celebration Publishers, 1991)

Chapter 12 - Healing in the Atonement

physical defect is thus guilty of their own affliction. Copeland notes,

> "Sometimes people won't receive their healing. Sometimes they're full of fear or doubt or unbelief, and they can't take what God is giving them."[102]

Shame on you, disabled person! It is your word-faith which heals you and your lack of faith that condemns you to a dysfunctional body. And, in that case, according to Fred Price, you are choosing to live in a body which is unfitting for God's use! He asininely quips,

> "How can you glorify God in your body, when it doesn't function right? How can you glorify God? How can He get glory when your body doesn't even work? What makes you think the Holy Ghost wants to live inside a body where He can't see out through the windows and He can't hear with the ears? What makes you think the Holy Spirit wants to live inside of a physical body where the limbs and the organs and the cells do not function right?"[103]

As offensive as it sounds, any doctrine which establishes fully that God *will heal any sick person* if they have enough faith, or if they ask correctly or if any other number of human-initiated scenarios are done "properly," is a doctrine which *makes the believer ultimately at fault for their own sicknesses.* Even more offensive is Price's notion that God would find such a body an uninhabitable vessel. Apparently, in Price's view, one who is physically

---

[102] **Kenneth Copeland** ("Believer's Voice Of Victory", October 1999, pg. 23).

[103] **Frederick K.C. Price** ("Is God Glorified Through Sickness?" audiotape #FP605).

disabled or diseased cannot even be redeemed! If the Holy Spirit wants no part of a broken body then salvation is unattainable for the blind, deaf and disabled at all, for the Holy Spirit is the agent of salvation and the indwelling Spirit of life which proceeds justification.

How would one explain this truth to Joni Ericson Tada, Tony Melendez or any of *thousands* of believers who serve God faithfully in spite of a debilitating illness or injury? Would the Holy Spirit *not want to live* inside the restricted body of a disabled person? Is their faith thus in vain? Have their physical maladies revealed their true estate of condemnation without Christ? Has he abandoned them to eternity in Hell?

The real question is clearly, "Are they false disciples or is Price?"

If such toxic voices were all that a disabled, injured or terminally ill person ever heard, the name of Christ would be profaned among all who suffer from such infirmities. Fortunately, by God's providence, a voice much louder, thoroughly tested and approved than the voices of Price, Copeland, Hinn, Osteen and all other human teachers exists to us in the scripture itself.

May every sick, injured or disabled person know that the Holy Spirit is perfectly content to live in what Price calls an essentially "dysfunctional" body. Indeed, there is no other type; for we all live in a temporal vessel of death and decay; including Fred Price. Some of these impostors who claim to never have a headache, toothache or muscle pain, are liars; plain and simple. Never has there been a sinful being devoid of physical infirmity. And, contrary to the teachings of the Word of Faith movement, the scripture does not claim that healing from every physical frailty is the right of the believer. It is – as are all other rights – the right of God himself. He will heal whom He will and He will inflict whom He will. Such is the truthful, biblical notion of sovereignty. Indeed, varying affliction has been granted continuance by God himself in some cases, such as none other than the Apostle Paul. He testifies clearly that,

> **2 Corinthians 12:7-10 (ESV)**
> [7] ... *to keep me from becoming conceited because of the surpassing greatness of the revelations, a thorn was given me in the flesh, a messenger of Satan to harass me, to keep me from becoming conceited.*
> [8] *Three times I pleaded with the Lord about this, that it should leave me.*
> [9] *But he said to me, "My grace is sufficient for you, for my power is made perfect in weakness." Therefore I will boast all the more gladly of my weaknesses, so that the power of Christ may rest upon me.*
> [10] *For the sake of Christ, then, I am content with weaknesses, insults, hardships, persecutions, and calamities. For when I am weak, then I am strong.*

In 2 Corinthians, Paul notes the receiving of a "thorn" in his flesh. The term "flesh" is the Greek term, *sarx,* which refers to the natural human body. Paul clearly does not speak of a literal thorn, but a metaphorical one. If it were merely a literal thorn he would simply remove it. He clearly had an ailment of some sort in his body which he is unable to remedy. We cannot know exactly what it was, but can clearly know that it was physical in nature. His body was afflicted. What is of vital significance is that *God chose to allow Paul to suffer with his ailment* rather than healing him from it. This is clearly in denial of the WoF teaching that healing is a God-given right for every believer. God did not tell Paul to "call out" his affliction or to speak faith filled words against it. He did not instruct Paul that his healing was granted in the atonement and he should simply claim it. In fact, God refused to heal Paul based on the premise that Paul could better serve God *with his affliction*!

God's providential stance on the subject was that, "*my grace is sufficient for you, for my power is made perfect in weakness.*" Clearly, God *wanted* Paul to have this particular ailment, as Paul noted, "*to keep me from becoming conceited*" from the great revelations God had allowed Paul to witness. As such, Paul's continuing affliction was a direct result of God's use in his life. Had Paul been of lesser consequence to God's program, it seems that God may have indeed healed him. But to keep Paul as God wanted him, unconceited in light of what God had shown him, Paul was thus required to carry a physical burden.

Far from the snooty notion of the spiritual elite having supremacy over their physical condition, Paul – a true spiritual giant – was rather satisfied and proud to endure it. Interestingly, Paul does not claim that the Holy Spirit would no longer want to use his defective body as His temple. He does not condemn himself for a lack of faith in speaking it away. Rather, he realizes his condition as a gift from God to make him more fitting for God's use. As Paul notes, "*I will boast all the more gladly of my weaknesses, so that the power of Christ may rest upon me.*" He continues, "*For the sake of Christ, then, I am content with weaknesses, insults, hardships, persecutions, and calamities. For when I am weak, then I am strong.*" This is how a true man of God understands his limitations and God-given suffering.

Contrary to Fred Price's deceptive anecdote, scripture teaches that God is actually *glorified* when a believer patiently endures suffering by depending on Christ's power to achieve that which their less than perfect bodies are unable to do for themselves. How dare Price to bring humility, accusation and disrespect to sanctified temples of the Holy Spirit; some of which could be experiencing *God's grace* in their suffering, as Paul did.

The sheer arrogance of defect demonstrated by WoF theology only continues to assert the real purpose of its teachers.

> **Titus 1:11 (ESV)**
> *¹¹ They must be silenced, since they are upsetting whole families by teaching for shameful gain what they ought not to teach.*

In the pursuit of that purpose, they have continually maligned God's word, character and sovereignty. They have ruined people who are physically hindered by sickness, injury or defect; leading them away from the only guaranteed healing any of us have hope for; an eternal one. How devastating to the legitimate body of Christ it is when its weak are destroyed for the sake of the wealthy counterfeits among them.

Chapter 13 – Guaranteed Wealth

Such arrogant insult is not limited to the physically restricted, sadly. The poor fall under similar condemnation for their financial status. Continuing their pursuit of self-serve theology, the next major assault of biblical theology in the WoF program concerns their warped doctrine of wealth. This dogma teaches that each believer in Christ should expect to be wealthy and have the absolute best of everything their culture offers. And to not be wealthy is perceived as a sure sign of spiritual failure. Price asserts,

> "Yeah, God has pleasure in the prosperity. So he must have displeasure in the poverty. So if he does, then poverty couldn't be from God. Yeah, but Brother Price, but God allows it. God lets it happen. You're right, he does. He does, because you do. He can't do anything about it."[104]

The essence of the WoF wealth doctrine begins, of course, with the idea that God *wants* his children all to be affluent, for according to these teachers, wealth is a God-given right to all who follow Christ. Hagin noted,

> "He wants His children to eat the best, He wants them to wear the best clothing, He wants them to drive the best cars, and He wants them to have the best of

---

[104] **Fred Price**, (Ever Increasing Faith 11/16/90).

everything."[105]

While such promises of wealth sound both appealing and desirable to a market-driven church shopper, they are utterly contrary to the teachings of scripture. The scriptures never assert that the essence of Christianity is worldly welfare. The Bible more commonly presents earthly pleasure as that which must be repented of for the gain of the spiritual.

Paul serves as a firm rebuttal witness to this incredulous reversal, as he says,

> *1 Timothy 6:6-11 (ESV)*
> *⁶ Now there is great gain in godliness with contentment,*
> *⁷ for we brought nothing into the world, and we cannot take anything out of the world.*
> *⁸ But if we have food and clothing, with these we will be content.*
> *⁹ But those who desire to be rich fall into temptation, into a snare, into many senseless and harmful desires that plunge people into ruin and destruction.*
> *¹⁰ For the love of money is a root of all kinds of evils. It is through this craving that some have wandered away from the faith and pierced themselves with many pangs.*
> *¹¹ But as for you, O man of God, flee these things. Pursue righteousness, godliness, faith, love, steadfastness, gentleness.*

According to Paul, God's children are to be content with food and clothing alone! And, contrary to Hagin's premise, Paul notes that the desire to get rich leads men into destruction, rather than God's good graces. He concludes the matter with the true biblical position

---

[105] **Kenneth Hagin, Sr.** (Quoted by D.L. McConnell, A Different Gospel p.175)

concerning the pursuit of wealth, "*but as for you, O man of God, flee these things. Pursue righteousness, godliness, faith, love, steadfastness, gentleness.*"

It is important to note that neither Paul, nor any other biblical writers teach that wealth is inherently evil, or that to have wealth necessarily indicates a sinful state. What Paul teaches, however, is quite contrary to the WoF position, namely that God wants everyone to be rich. Paul teaches that what God wants is for everyone to be *content* with what he has provided for them. One's pursuit is not to be oriented toward riches, but righteousness, godliness, faith, love, endurance and gentleness. What an enigma it is that men who tout multi-million dollar mansions, private jets and $10,000 suits as spiritual badges of honor claim to serve a man who was crucified with nothing but the clothes on his back. Yet, having riches is exceptionally important to the WoF dogma; for such a doctrine alone can conceal the deep corruption of greed that represents the true motivation of its teachers. If having worldly riches can be masqueraded as spiritual virtue then lavishly wealthy offenders of the faith appear as super apostles rather than corrupt and worldly charlatans; which suits their desires quite nicely all around.

The continual conjecture of these false shepherds is that God pays outstanding temporal benefits to those who serve him. Fred Price goes so far as to insinuate that believers are essentially on God's payroll, and should *expect* a financial reward from their service to God. He retorts that,

> "most employers at least have enough common decency about them that they don't ask somebody to work for *them for free*.... If a man has enough nicety about him to do that, can't you at least believe that the Father God is not asking you to serve Him for free

either?"[106]

To "*serve him for free???*" Does Price have *no understanding* of the gospel of Christ? Does he truly believe that God *owes us something?* Indeed, God does, but it is certainly not a reward. The scriptures exclaim boldly that what man is owed by God is the penalty of eternal death for the wages of his sin. A true believer in Christ does not serve God for free *or* for pay, but as an outpouring of response to God's mercy. Because God has *not* given us what we have earned - the wages of sin - Romans says,

> **Romans 12:1 (ESV)**
> [1] *I appeal to you therefore, brothers, by the mercies of God, to present your bodies as a living sacrifice, holy and acceptable to God, which is your spiritual worship.*

Our service to God is not portrayed in scripture as a means to a financial end. Service is a *response* to God's exceptional mercy! He saved believers from an eternal destiny of destruction and Hell, which is all we have ever earned from him. In spite of this, God so loved the world that he sent Jesus to die on a cross to pay for our sins. How can one's service to God be considered as "free" by anyone who truly understands the nature of God's grace toward sinners? Service to God is the believer's spiritual act of worship, or as the KJV states it, "*your reasonable service.*" Worship, or service to God, is a *response to His grace*, not an occupation which yields a wage. God's gift of eternal life has already been accepted by his true worshippers, and it can *never* be repaid by one's service. Such claims clearly identify these teachers as outcasts

---

[106] **Fred Price**, (D.L. McConnell p.170 op. cit. F. Price Faith, Foolishness, presumption p.7)

from God's glory, as the scripture notes that to preach service to God as a means to financial gain is the biblical marker of a false teacher!

> *1 Timothy 6:3-5 (ESV)*
> *³ If anyone teaches a different doctrine and does not agree with the sound words of our Lord Jesus Christ and the teaching that accords with godliness,*
> *⁴ he is puffed up with conceit and understands nothing. He has an unhealthy craving for controversy and for quarrels about words, which produce envy, dissension, slander, evil suspicions,*
> *⁵ and constant friction among people who are depraved in mind and deprived of the truth,* **imagining that godliness is a means of gain.**

Price, Hinn, Copeland and every other WoF teacher that presents the gospel paycheck anomaly are quite aggressively revealing who they truly are. The scripture does not issue such warnings to be ignored. By proclaiming service to God as sound financial principle, they have firmly established to the true church that they are frauds. Paul minces no words in his condemnation of such a sentiment. They are "*depraved in mind*," and "*deprived of the truth.*"

Yet, this text doesn't begin to hinder prosperity preachers from dictating contrary doctrines out of their extra-biblical sources. Rather, they proliferate at inventing doctrinal reversals of the clear teaching of scripture. Hinn notes that,

> "poverty is from the devil and that God wants all Christians prosperous."[107]

---

[107] **Benny Hinn**, (TBN broadcast, 11/6/90)

Friends, *any teacher*, including myself, Billy Graham or John Calvin, should establish their teachings on the basis of biblical exegesis. The very definition of preaching and teaching within the confines of Protestantism necessitates that an instructor present that which comes from *the Bible*, rather than from their minds, culture, historical hand-me-downs or other extra-biblical sources. To teach that which is added to the Bible, once again, is the essence of the definition of a cult.

These teachers practice such a cultic methodology by depending on their own unverifiable dreams, visits from God and personal agendas, using scripture as support material rather than the benchmark of truth. In true biblical preaching, scripture is the standard of faith and the end of all doctrinal presumption. When scripture becomes secondary to one's own message, it has been relegated to the realms of illustration, poems and stories. In such cases, they have defined themselves as Paul warned; those who teach *"a different doctrine"* which *"does not agree with the sound words of our Lord."*

An obvious objection to such outlandish assertions from the true source of scripture would be the person of Christ himself, the apostles and early church who are regularly noted in scripture to be poor; even to extreme circumstance.[108] Ironically, a major supposed "support" for the WoF wealth doctrines comes from the attempt to recast Jesus as having been a very wealthy man. As Prices says it,

> "The whole point is I'm trying to get you to see--to get you out of this malaise of thinking that Jesus and the disciples were poor and then relating that to you-

---

[108] 2 Corinthians 8:2, Revelation 2:9, Philippians 4:12

thinking that you, as a child of God, have to follow Jesus. The Bible says that He has left us an example that we should follow His steps. That's the reason why I drive a Rolls Royce. I'm following Jesus' steps."[109]

Price at least seems to understand that one is to follow Jesus' model. Sadly, he has no concept of what that truth reveals. According to him and virtually every other popular WoF teacher the church has historically misunderstood Jesus' financial status. Jesus, according to faulty interpretive standards, is regularly promoted as one who lived out a very well-funded and lavish lifestyle.

John Avanzini goes the extra mile on this fanatical deception, damaging at least three different biblical texts by falsifying them into their *exact polar opposite* that he may teach Jesus was rich. He preaches that,

> Jesus had a nice house, a big house - big enough to have company stay the night with Him at the house. Let me show you His house. Go over to John the first chapter and I'll show you His house.... Now, child of God, that's a house big enough to have company stay the night in. There's His house."[110]

This first ignorant example is Avanzini's deduction that Jesus was rich because, as he contends, Jesus had a nice, big house. Avanzini invites us to challenge him via the rarely seen citation of a chapter and verse. I do appreciate that change of pace. An actual biblical quote will surely suffice as evidence to the trustworthiness of his claim. He should, however, have resorted to revelation knowledge

---

[109] **Frederick K.C. Price** (Ever Increasing Faith, TBN December 9, 1990)

[110] **John Avanzini** (Believer's Voice of Victory, TBN January 20, 1991)

on this one. The scriptures simply refute every aspect of his position.

Avanzini's reference to Jesus' theoretical house is only mentioned in the book of John, which notes,

> **John 1:35-39 (ESV)**
> [35] The next day again John was standing with two of his disciples,
> [36] and he looked at Jesus as he walked by and said, "Behold, the Lamb of God!"
> [37] The two disciples heard him say this, and they followed Jesus.
> [38] Jesus turned and saw them following and said to them, "What are you seeking?" And they said to him, "Rabbi" (which means Teacher), "where are you staying?"
> [39] He said to them, "Come and you will see." So they came and saw where he was staying, and they stayed with him that day, for it was about the tenth hour.

Avanzini's conclusions are threefold from this text. First, he presumes that Jesus had a house. He then surmises that it was a large house, and lastly, by some unknown method he concludes that it had to have been a "nice" house. John 1 teaches absolutely no conclusion that Avanzini professes. It is certainly clear from the text that Jesus was staying somewhere. But, the question asked of Jesus in verse 38 is not "do you own a house," but rather, "*where are you staying.*" To answer such a question with "*come and you will see*" is by no means tantamount to proof of ownership of a home. The text only asserts that Jesus was staying somewhere. It does not assert that the location *belonged* to Jesus, or that it was large and luxurious. My children do not own a house, but *they stay* in *my* house freely. Such was the likely nature of Jesus' stay in this house, but certainly there is no assertion as to Jesus owning the house. Jesus was an itinerate preacher. Jewish law required that traveling guests be accommodated. As such, he would likely have had a house to sleep in on any given night. *"Come and you will see"* merely indicates that Jesus led these men to that location.

Additionally, there is irrefutably nothing in the text that indicates the *niceness* of neither the home where he stayed, nor anything which depicts the size of the home. Verse 37 states that two men went to stay with Jesus that day, not specifically indicating whether they stayed the night or not. Assuming that they *did* stay the night, just how large does a home need to be to accompany *two additional men*? Could not a 500 square foot efficiency apartment in the South Bronx accommodate *two additional people* for an evening? What about a pop-up camper, for crying out loud? Aside from the fact that *this was not Jesus' home,* it is an asinine presumption to conclude a home to be "large" and/or "nice" because two additional men *may have* stayed an evening in it. A grass hut in the poorest African village could accommodate the same and more.

The true tragedy of Avanzini's assertion yet lies more clearly in scripture than his fantasy gives clue. For far more important than Avanzini's egregious eisegesis (reading into the text) are Jesus' own words on the subject. In Matthew,

> **Matthew 8:19-20 (ESV)**
> [19] *... a scribe came up and said to him, "Teacher, I will follow you wherever you go."*
> [20] *And Jesus said to him, "Foxes have holes, and birds of the air have nests, but the Son of Man has nowhere to lay his head."*

In response to a disciple offering to travel with Jesus, his comment was simple, "*the Son of Man has nowhere to lay his head.*" Without question, Jesus warns this disciple that he had no home, and that following him is no picnic.

Jesus certainly had accommodations that he frequented, such as Peter's and Lazarus' homes, but he personally had no home of his own; the fictitious sign of wealth proposed by Avanzini.[111] As with every other WoF postulate, one must only decide whether to believe Jesus' testimony or Avanzini's on a given subject. If Jesus had a home then he was truly deceptive about it, but I'm firmly more confident that Avanzini is the deceiver among the two.

A second infamous Avanzini perjury concerning Jesus' supposed wealth involves some truly adventurous biblical navigation. Once again, it is nice to have a scriptural reference, at least, yet Avanzini clearly has issues with his interpretive method, for he notes that,

> "John 19 tells us that Jesus wore designer clothes. Well, what else you gonna call it? Designer clothes - that's blasphemy. No, that's what we call them today. I mean, you didn't get the stuff He wore off the rack. It wasn't a one-size-fits-all deal. No, this was custom stuff. It was the kind of garment that kings and rich merchants wore. Kings and rich merchants wore that garment."[112]

Sadly, what Avanzini refers to is nothing short of a mockery of Jesus' shame on the cross. Fulfilling the prophecy of Psalm 22:18, Roman soldiers divided Jesus' clothing among themselves at his crucifixion.

> *John 19:23-24 (ESV)*
> *²³ When the soldiers had crucified Jesus, they took his garments and divided them into four parts, one part for each soldier; also his tunic. But the tunic was*

---

[111] Luke 4:38, John 12:1

[112] **John Avanzini** (Believer's Voice of Victory, TBN January 20, 1991)

Apostasy! | 177

seamless, woven in one piece from top to bottom, ²⁴ *so they said to one another, "Let us not tear it, but cast lots for it to see whose it shall be." This was to fulfill the Scripture which says, "They divided my garments among them, and for my clothing they cast lots." So the soldiers did these things,*

In the context of Jesus' crucifixion, as was customary, the soldiers took the clothing of the victims for themselves. In Jesus' case, only one garment was noted to be special; his undergarment. The other clothes were distributed without issue, but the undergarment was noted to indeed be unique. It "*was seamless, woven in one piece from top to bottom.*"

Indeed, scripture teaches that Jesus did have a very nice undergarment. It was apparently beautifully and artistically made. Avanzini's assertion that "it wasn't a one-size-fits-all deal" only communicates his lack of knowledge of historical biblical backgrounds. Surely Avanzini pays a premium for his tailor-made clothing. However, *all clothing was hand-made in those days*. None of it was likely to have come "off the rack," but rather from a family member whose job was to make clothing for the household. To have a garment which was unique by merit of its being "*woven in one piece from top to bottom*" speaks not to the expense of it, but rather the care and craftsmanship of its maker. Mary or any other woman in Jesus' family would most likely have made this garment. Its uniqueness speaks only to the skill and possibly the time invested in its construction, however. It states nothing of the expense of the materials. Yes, it was *custom made,* as most all garments were in that day. Yet, the portrait of Jesus getting measured for an Armani suit fit for a WoF TV preacher is not being depicted in the text whatsoever. How evident it is that a privileged huckster is masquerading as a servant of the living God when he equates a handmade item of Jesus' day to a tailor made designer garment that he may wear while riding in his Rolls to a TBN Telethon. It defies logic that such ignorance is discounted and embraced as truth in this movement.

Avanzini's third claim to Jesus' wealth is what he understands to be the fruits of Jesus' supposedly affluent ministry. Indeed, it must be hard for a man like Avanzini to imagine Jesus having so many followers and not be incredibly wealthy. He educates his TBN fans that,

> "Jesus was handling big money because that treasurer he had was a thief. Now you can't tell me that a ministry with a treasurer that's a thief can operate on a few pennies. It took big money to operate that ministry because Judas was stealing out of that bag. If you have a treasurer that means you have a lot of money."[113]

Yet again, Avanzini surmises an incredibly shoddy conclusion: surely "big money" was at stake for anyone with a thieving treasurer.

To have a treasurer simply denotes that a person has been assigned the responsibility of keeping the finances of a group. It in no way demands a certain sum of money to exist, but only an accountable party to have been established to oversee cash flow; however large or small. Boy Scout troops and community watches have treasurers. They certainly would not be construed to be handling "big money" for that reason alone.

Likewise, to have a treasurer who is a thief speaks not at all concerning the size of the sum of money in hand. It merely indicates the acquisition of a dishonest treasurer. A treasurer who steals $5 from a $50 kitty is as much of a

---

[113] **John Avanzini** (Praise the Lord, TBN, September 15, 1988)

thief as one who embezzles millions from the government. Being "a thief" is not defined by a compulsory dollar amount which one must have stolen. A thief, by definition, is one who takes something which does not belong to him; regardless of the amount. Surely Avanzini couldn't imagine stealing anything less than millions, but such was in no wise ever indicated by the testimony of scripture concerning Christ's ministry purse.

Ironically, Avanzini's reference to Judas' greed serves more to prove that Jesus' itinerate ministry *did not* have big financial stakes, for Judas gave up his ongoing treasury theft for a singular payout of thirty silver coins. Scripture declares that,

> **Matthew 26:14-15 (ESV)**
> *[14] ... one of the twelve, whose name was Judas Iscariot, went to the chief priests*
> *[15] and said, "What will you give me if I deliver him over to you?" And they paid him thirty pieces of silver.*

It is unclear what denomination these coins were, as the text only relates "silver coins." If the coins were denari, the full thirty pieces would be worth a month's salary. It very well may have been another coin as well. However, after Judas returned the money the chief priests took the money and bought a field in which to bury strangers.[114] Even then it is unknown how large a field was purchased. Yet I find myself asking, would enough money to buy a field be considered "big money" to Avanzini? Not likely, unless the field in question was a California beachfront containing a mansion and yacht slip. Why, then, would Judas give up the fantasized "big money" of Jesus' treasury to sell out for 30 pieces of silver?

---

[114] Matthew 27:3-10

Another consideration concerning the 30 silver pieces is that Matthew's Jewish readers would have readily understood the value of 30 pieces of silver to equate to the compensatory price of a slave *some fifteen hundred years earlier* in accordance to the Law of Moses.

> **Exodus 21:32 (ESV)**
> [32] *If the ox gores a slave, male or female, the owner shall give to their master thirty shekels of silver, and the ox shall be stoned.*

Thus, by all potential biblical consideration, Jesus was sold cheap by Judas; the price of a common slave – or of a field to bury dead in. Judas, as an acknowledged thief, was clearly an opportunist. He would have stolen in accordance to that which would have been most profitable to him. It makes no logical sense that he was regularly stealing from a pot of "big money" yet sold Jesus for 30 pieces of silver.

As such, Avanzini's weak attempt to portray Jesus as a rock-star world-touring wealthy pastor type in his own image fails miserably according to God's word. Scripture teaches quite contrary to any assertion of Jesus' wealth at all, rather proclaiming that Jesus was in fact, quite poor.

Even from birth, scripture notes Christ as having been designated by God to be raised by virtual paupers. Mary and Joseph can legitimately be labeled as poor people by the biblical account of Jesus' birth.

> **Luke 2:22-24 (ESV)**
> [22] *And when the time came for their purification according to the Law of Moses, they brought him up to Jerusalem to present him to the Lord*
> [23] *(as it is written in the Law of the Lord, "Every male who first opens the womb shall be called holy to the Lord")*
> [24] *and to offer a sacrifice according to what is said in*

the Law of the Lord, "a pair of turtledoves, or two young pigeons."

Jesus' parents offered a pair of doves for Mary's purification. Under normal circumstances, according to the Law, one would offer up a lamb for purification rites after birth. Yet, Luke informs the reader that Joseph and Mary gave either doves or pigeons, the offering *of the poor* according to the Law of Moses. The legal requirement Luke speaks of notes that after birth, the priest should make an offering of a lamb,

> ***Leviticus 12:7-8 (ESV)***
> *[7] ... before the LORD and make atonement for her. Then she shall be clean from the flow of her blood. This is the law for her who bears a child, either male or female.*
> *[8] And if she cannot afford a lamb, then she shall take two turtledoves or two pigeons, one for a burnt offering and the other for a sin offering. And the priest shall make atonement for her, and she shall be clean.*

A lamb is the normal offering. Only if the mother is too poor to afford a lamb is she allowed by the Law to offer doves or pigeons. Mary, clearly, was just such a woman. She was very poor.

It is also worthy to note that Jesus was buried in another – truly rich - man's tomb rather than one of his own.[115] Jesus clearly had knowledge of his pending death. He had warned the disciples no less than three times that he would be killed, buried and raised.[116] If Jesus had "big money," would he have not purchased a tomb for his family under such circumstances? There are many more biblical references concerning the life of Christ that

---

[115] Matthew 27:57-60

[116] Matthew 16:21, Matthew 17:22-23, Matthew 20:18-19

illustrate his poverty than even Avanzini can make up to artificially demonstrate his wealth. Every scriptural teaching which hints at Jesus' financial position is consistent. He was the son of a poor carpenter who conducted a three year itinerant preaching ministry during which time he had neither home nor a regular income beyond the donations of some of his followers. He died with only one possession of noted envy; a nicely woven undergarment.

Jesus was not rich. Any attempt by the super-affluent stars of the WoF to paint him as such is nothing less than a diversion from their own corrupt and decadent natures. Such is a necessary step to add credibility to their lavish lifestyle, without which, they would have no reason to continue in counterfeit ministry. They have painstakingly accommodated themselves via this wealth doctrine, claiming not only that Jesus was wealthy, but he raised up a group of apostles that followed in his financially prosperous footsteps. Fred Price claims,

> "The apostles were businessmen. They were rich men (and) had plenty of money. I'm going to show you that Jesus was a wealthy man, had plenty of money and see all of that completely foreign to us from a traditional point of view...." "Jesus and the disciples were rich. Only rich people could take off for three and a half years."[117]

Price poses a deceptive hypothesis, although speaking it as if it were truth. "Only rich people could take off for three and a half years." I'm sure this seems clever to Price, who certainly *could* take off for 3.5 years, which would benefit everyone. Yet, this quote only serves to

---

[117] **Frederick K.C. Price** (Ever Increasing Faith, TBN, November 23, 1990)

demonstrate Price's misunderstanding of the very nature of the calling of the apostles: a characteristic he could not begin to comprehend. The simple fact is that they *chose to quit their jobs*, follow Christ and *be poor*! Their quitting work and following Christ speaks not of their wealth, but rather of their lack of the love of money, something no WoF preacher could have ever guessed, so far is it from their appreciation. Scripture notes,

> **Matthew 4:18-20 (ESV)**
> [18] *While walking by the Sea of Galilee, he saw two brothers, Simon (who is called Peter) and Andrew his brother, casting a net into the sea, for they were fishermen.*
> [19] *And he said to them, "Follow me, and I will make you fishers of men."*
> [20] *Immediately they left their nets and followed him.*

Peter and John were fishermen. They were common, blue collar worker bees, who left their boats, nets and money making ability on the ground to follow Jesus. Likewise, James and John shared the same occupation prior to their ministry with Christ.

> **Matthew 4:21-22 (ESV)**
> [21] *And going on from there he saw two other brothers, James the son of Zebedee and John his brother, in the boat with Zebedee their father, mending their nets, and he called them.*
> [22] *Immediately they left the boat and their father and followed him.*

Just how wealthy does Price think these first century fishermen were? If they were "rich enough to take off three and a half years," would they not be rich enough to have hired out the running of their businesses? Would the single boat they left behind be the boat of their father? Clearly they were simple tradesmen in family businesses. They were not corporate moguls who left massive salaries and pensions on hold.

Matthew was a tax collector, and *may* have in fact been wealthy at the time Jesus called him, as *may* have been Luke, who was a doctor. Yet, these men *gave up their incomes* to follow Jesus. Avanzini and Price consider that following Jesus is a means to financial gain, but never stop to realize that the men who followed Jesus in scripture *gave up* their funding in order to be itinerate. I wonder if Avanzini, Price, Copeland and Hinn would give up their wealth and preach free for a few years? They are all certainly wealthy enough to do so. The reason they do not - and never will - is not that they do not have enough money. It is because of their *love for money*. Their greed would never allow them to preach for free. The disciples' lack of the love for money is precisely why they were willing to leave their jobs, travel through Israel and preach for free.

Avanzini further references the later years of the apostles, asserting that successful and financially bloated ministries were attributed to them after the time of Christ. He states,

> "Paul had the kind of money that could stop up justice."[118]

Yet, Paul testified quite the opposite about himself and the other apostles.

> *1 Corinthians 4:10-12 (ESV)*
> *[10] We are fools for Christ's sake, but you are wise in Christ. We are weak, but you are strong. You are held in honor, but we in disrepute.*
> *[11] To the present hour we hunger and thirst, we are poorly dressed and buffeted and homeless,*
> *[12] and we labor, working with our own hands....*

---

[118] **John Avanzini** (Believer's Voice of Victory, TBN, January 20, 1991)

Apostasy! | 185

Does Avanzini know Paul better than Paul knows himself? In Paul's own testimony, he was *hungry, thirsty, was poorly dressed, hard working, persecuted and homeless!* Apparently he didn't have designer clothes, either, because he preached for free. It was for this reason that Paul kept a secondary occupation to pay for his bills.[119] How can one presume to be a Christian teacher and make such outlandish assertions in clear denial of the scriptures? Perhaps the more important question should be, "What is the purpose of attempting to reconstruct Jesus and the disciples as wealthy?" The answer to that question should be crystal clear at this point. These men depend on a doctrine of wealth to justify their own excessive and frivolous lifestyles. And, in order for them to continue to live lavishly, a doctrine of wealth must be seen as godly and proper. As such, they continue to note that God's desire is for all of his faithful servants to be wealthy.

And, as these teachers are prone to do, they take such a stance to its logical conclusion. Simply put, they faithfully preach that if one is not wealthy, they have denied their birthright in Christ and are thus living in sin. Rod Parsley proclaims,

> "For you to sit in physical bondage is to deny the power of the gospel. Most people would have no trouble shouting whatsoever if I said, "To remain in the bondage of sin and death is to deny the power of the gospel." If I said the same thing about poverty and financial bondage, it would get as quiet as a tomb. If I said that for you to live from paycheck to paycheck is to deny the power of the gospel, many of you would get angry. In Luke 4:18, Notice there was an anointing

---

[119] 1 Corinthians 9:1-18, Acts 18:1-3

> to preach good news to the poor. A lot of people don't like to look at that because good news to a poor man is that he doesn't have to be poor anymore. We have multitudes saved, delivered and filled with the Holy Ghost, and many are healed, yet over 90% of the church of Jesus Christ are living in absolute financial bondage. All the while, Jesus is saying, "I've been anointed to preach the good news to the poor." You have held back the flow. You have denied the perpetual propulsion of power that could deliver you from not only sin and sickness but from the horrible stench of poverty."[120]

It is almost painful to have to rebuke such rubbish. Parsley can't begin to make sense of the most obvious doctrinal references. His supposed biblical mandate for every believer to be rich is Jesus' quote of the Messianic prophecy of Isaiah 61, which notes,

> **Luke 4:18 (ESV)**
> [18] *"The Spirit of the Lord is upon me, because he has anointed me to proclaim good news to the poor. He has sent me to proclaim liberty to the captives and recovering of sight to the blind, to set at liberty those who are oppressed...."*

How revealing it is that Parsley thinks "good news to a poor man is that he doesn't have to be poor anymore." How anyone can doubt his motivation is a true mystery.

Those of us who read our Bibles for reasons other than the discovery of talking points for our multi-million dollar apostate church "business" understand this text on a profoundly deeper level than Parsley is capable. The term translated "preach good news" is the Greek word,

---

[120] **Rod Parsley** *God's Answer to Insufficient Funds* (Canal Winchester: World Harvest Church, 1992) 46-47

euangelizo, which means "preach the good news" in a context that relates to the rich and poor alike. Certainly the context was not fully understood when Isaiah penned the reference, but Christ came to bring meaning to the "good news" Isaiah spoke of. *Euangelizo* is the word from which we derive our English terms "evangelism" and "gospel." Jesus noted that he was coming to *evangelize the poor.* As such, "poor" does not refer to those who are financially bankrupt, but *spiritually* so. Perhaps these men have never heard of the good news; better known as "the gospel?" This is what *euangelizo* refers to in the New Testament. *Euangelizo* is the term Peter used in Acts 15:7 noting that, *"the Gentiles should hear the word of the gospel and believe."* It is this same term that Peter asks, *"what will be the outcome for those who do not obey the gospel of God?"*[121] This term is what Paul used when he noted that some other disciple's *"conduct was not in step with the truth of the gospel."*[122] This term, used 77 times in the New Testament, is our term for "evangelize," when used as a verb, which means "the proclaiming of the gospel." When used as a noun, it simply means "gospel," or "good news." Good news, or the gospel, to a poor man is that Christ died for his sins so he can be forgiven – *not that "he doesn't have to be poor anymore"* in a financial sense. Only a truly corrupt mind could present such a juvenile misrepresentation of the biblical text with a straight face.

Parsley notes further that living paycheck to paycheck is denying the power of the gospel. Surely living in this manner may be unbiblical, as one should offer stewardship of his income more properly than such if

---

[121] 1 Peter 4:17

[122] Galatians 2:14

possible. Yet, "the power of the gospel" has nothing to do with financial increase except to those who hold to a Word of Faith premise. Parsley's contention is that if one lacks financial means he has "held back the flow. You have denied the perpetual propulsion of the power that could deliver you…from the horrible stench of poverty." Is this what WoF teachers think the gospel is all about? Did Jesus leave Heaven, come to earth and die on a cross so that believers could have money?

Such nonsense is in stark opposition to the true gospel of Christ. James noted,

> **James 1:9-10 (ESV)**
> [9] Let the lowly brother boast in his exaltation,
> [10] and the rich in his humiliation, because like a flower of the grass he will pass away.

James' assertion is that it is the poor who are exalted. The rich, for all of their hope in their wealth, will wither away like the grass. He further asserts that we *should not show favoritism to the rich*, for

> **James 2:5-7 (ESV)**
> [5] …has not God chosen those who are poor in the world to be rich in faith and heirs of the kingdom, which he has promised to those who love him?
> [6] But you have dishonored the poor man. Are not the rich the ones who oppress you, and the ones who drag you into court?
> [7] Are they not the ones who blaspheme the honorable name by which you were called?

So radical is James' opinion of the rich that some have accused him of unfairly judging them in his epistle. It is clearly preferable to James to be poor materially so that one can properly focus upon being rich in the faith. Is such not what Jesus meant when he said,

> **Luke 18:24-25 (ESV)**
> [24] Jesus, seeing that he had become sad, said, "How

difficult it is for those who have wealth to enter the kingdom of God! ²⁵ *For it is easier for a camel to go through the eye of a needle than for a rich person to enter the kingdom of God."*

Jesus proclaimed that riches are a deterrent from the gospel, not the substance of it. One might expect a perversion of scripture to lead to the conclusion that *being rich* is a sin rather than being poor! Scripture does not teach this, yet it comes far closer to teaching such than it does to teaching that poverty is a sin.

In spite of a wealth of biblical evidence to the contrary, WoF teachers are addicted to this premise. The natural conclusion of such a cockeyed doctrine comes once again full circle to the word-faith mantra. If being poor is the natural state and being wealthy is the spiritual conclusion of the gospel, then one must find the source of such wealth inherent in their gospel understanding.

Sadly, the easiest way to become rich seems to be for one to begin a teaching ministry on TBN. Perhaps new believers should begin to make up doctrines that tickle the ears of this world and write books about them. That practice has certainly generated wealth for these teachers, but such is not the instruction for the student. WoF teachers frankly do not desire the competition. Instead, a believer's wealth inheritance is taught to originate from two other sources: speaking the Word of Faith, and giving generously to the ministry of the WoF teacher.

Of the first form of payout, Marilyn Hickey is quick to rehearse her students on the methodology, as noted earlier in this work.

> "What do you need? Start creating it. Start speaking about it. Start speaking it into being. Speak to your billfold. Say, "You big, thick billfold full of money."

> Speak to your checkbook. Say, "You, checkbook, you. You've never been so prosperous since I owned you. You're just jammed full of money."[123]

As with all other areas of WoF doctrine, when all else fails, the pronouncement of the word of faith will come to your rescue. As Kenyon stated, "what I confess I possess," is the battle call for one's miracle to form. Apparently, with the proper application of this method, money magically appears in one's empty wallet! For the record, I've tried this on stage in front of a live body of witnesses. It does not work. Likewise, the sold out halls of WoF telethon-style wealth-generating productions have left entire masses of disappointed and bankrupt people behind. But the false preaching tours are six towns away before their promised financial miracle fails to materialize for their supporters.

Copeland confirms the Word-Faith method as truth.

> "What you are saying is exactly what you are getting now. If you are living in poverty and lack and want, change what you are saying. The powerful force of the spiritual world that creates the circumstances around us is controlled by the words of the mouth."[124]

Just as healing is presumed to be manifest by words, so is one's financial position. Indeed, anything one desires can be created by the word-faith method according to the legend. Ironically the scriptures teach a simpler and much nobler approach to financial security. Primarily, it seems that God considers one's financial position to be somehow

---

[123] **Marilyn Hickey** (Claim Your Miracles audiotape #186, side 2)

[124] **Ken Copeland** *The Laws of Prosperity* (Fort Worth: Kenneth Copeland Publications, 1974) 98

tied to one's work ethic and stewardship. Paul, very contrary to the say and pay methodology, says,

> **Ephesians 4:28 (ESV)**
> [28] Let the thief no longer steal, but rather let him labor, doing honest work with his own hands, so that he may have something to share with anyone in need.

Teaching the church about principles of a transformed life in Christ, he requires a concept somewhat foreign to these teachers that a man "work with his own hands, so that he may have something to share." Likewise, the Proverbs note that,

> **Proverbs 10:4 (ESV)**
> [4] A slack hand causes poverty, but the hand of the diligent makes rich.

And Jesus notes the fruit of a wise investment in his parable of the talents. Of the foolish servant he notes,

> **Matthew 25:26-27 (ESV)**
> [26] ... 'You wicked and slothful servant! You knew that I reap where I have not sown and gather where I scattered no seed?
> [27] Then you ought to have invested my money with the bankers, and at my coming I should have received what was my own with interest.

What a novel idea the scriptures seem to reveal: work hard, invest and spend wisely. Such seems hardly fitting for the lifestyles of the rich and famous Word of Faith teacher. To them, money is a means to self-gratification and should be gained through the utterance of unbiblical mantras.

The second purported way one is able to attain their fiscal payout from the Lord is to support the "ministry" of one of his faithful WoF preachers. After all, such is the genuine point of the entire sham; to put money in the pockets of the sheerer. Those who support their local

Chapter 13 – Guaranteed Wealth

WoF ministry are noted to be unleashing a kernel of faith, for which the Lord will reward them generously. Such has been designated as "seed-faith," a term better known by most WoF students than "justification." The TBN newsletter has used such ploys to an excess. One example:

> "Do you have a need? God's law is simple and clear: Plant a seed - just like God did when He had a need. God needed sons and daughters, so He planted His very best - His only begotten Son - God could not have given more! As we have taught often, what did He receive? You know: MILLIONS of sons and daughters. Give God a seed - your best - and watch Him meet your need, great or small."[125]

Apparently, another of God's unwritten "laws" is known commonly by the TBN campaign crew. The law is simply, "plant a seed and God will meet your need."

Or, as Rod Parsley says it,

> "Ask your biggest need, go to the phone and put a seed to your need!"[126]

Perhaps at this point those of an innocent mindset could find themselves confused. What exactly is this "seed" that one is to plant? Do you really have to ask?

> "If people make the 2000 dollar faith pledge to TBN, not only will God give them the 2000 dollars before the year 2000 but he will also make them totally debt free and their whole family will be saved before the

---

[125] **TBN Newsletter** - (August 4, 2004)

[126] (Rod Parsley, TBN, Praise-A-Thon, March 31, 2004)

year 2000."[127]

Shambach's pledge goes even to the point of "assured salvation," a shameless ploy that hasn't seen the light of day this brazenly since Tetzel. The "seed" in question is, of course, cold hard cash (or credit cards suffice in most cases).

There is no mistake in the assertion: God can be bribed into meeting your financial needs and granting salvation to your whole family by a contribution to Trinity Broadcasting Network. One who is unschooled in the tactic may think that such a teaching encourages "giving for greed." Certainly the promise of riches in exchange for support to TBN fits the mold. Yet, according to Jesse Duplantis, it is not greedy at all to harvest from this tit-for-tat compensational model. It is in fact, just!

> "If I give $1,000 I deserve to get back $100,000 because I am just; that's not greed!"[128]

I suppose, for one who thinks Jesus died for the financial considerations of the poor; such truly might be construed as justification after all. At any rate, it is not considered greedy in this movement to give in the attitude of "deserving" a financial recompense from God. Nor is such a practice considered giving with a wrong motive, as Meyer notes,

> "Giving doesn't cost, it pays!"[129]

This raises perhaps the most logical question of all concerning the WoF teachers' wealth principles. If their

---

[127] (R.W. Shambach, Praise The Lord, TBN, Nov. 2, 1999)

[128] Jesse Duplantis ("The Just Shall Live By Faith", TBN, December 19, 2003)

[129] (Joyce Meyer, Daystar Spring Share-A-Thon, March 2, 2004)

doctrines are true, *why do they have to ask people to give at all?* Are they not empowered by the word of their faith to create *their own* wealth? Why do they insist on building it from their self-acknowledged cash-strapped audience? If, like Marilyn Hickey, they are able to simply "speak to [their] wallets," why do they not do so and leave the innocent and ignorant that trust them for spiritual answers quite enough alone?

The answer to that question is the answer to the entire dilemma of the WoF movement. This movement exists purely as the most expansive Ponzi scheme the world has ever encountered.

Chapter 14 - The Biblical Response

The nature of such schemes is that they only work if the promised returns are lucrative enough. Sadly, some arrive in a Word of Faith church or meeting due to a genuine desire to quench a spiritual longing. Christ, who fulfills that longing, is sufficient to lead them to a true gospel. However many flock to the Word of Faith movement for different reasons altogether. Promises of wealth, health and personal empowerment are expertly marketed to a materialistic culture which is drawn to such appeal. For that reason, the WoF message is sculpted very precisely so as to attract the target prey to its bait.

As noted in chapter 3, the modern church growth model is a particularly enticing concept; especially for a false teacher who has no vested interest in the kingdom of God otherwise. Such a model initiates numeric "church growth" by building, facilitating and selling a spiritual product desired by its target audience. Such was the nature of Paul's earlier noted warning to Timothy:

> *2 Timothy 4:3-4 (ESV)*
> *³ For the time is coming when people will not endure sound teaching, but having itching ears they will accumulate for themselves teachers to suit their own passions,*
> *⁴ and will turn away from listening to the truth and wander off into myths.*

This text has seen fruition in the current age like never before. Concerning the mentality of this apostasy, Paul made several assertions. First, he notes the commercialization of the Word of God. He says that *"people will not endure sound teaching,"* but will instead choose those which suits their own passions. Such is the nature of consumerism. If I want a blue car, I have no need to settle for another color, for blue ones are readily available. If likewise, I want to serve a God who lives to please *me*, I can make such a perceived choice as well, for men are readily available who will peddle such a gospel to my ears. Thus, it is the desire of man himself which will orient doctrines in this coming apostate age. Perhaps such is the greatest legitimate downfall to traditional capitalism: it has found its way into the spiritual arena, even to the local church. What man desires to hear as "truth" will thus find its way to a competing church arena.

It is further noted in the text that men "will accumulate" such teachers to provide such self-tailored theological services. As such, it is clear that a growing numerical quantity of people will desire to hear made-to-order doctrines, and will give validation to the false teachers which propagate them. It is at this point the reader should take great caution concerning the nature of how religious truth is noted to be validated in our culture.

Capitalistic societies have a natural tendency to assume that if a product produces satisfied customers, it must be good merchandise. Yet, simply because the masses affirm something to be true, it does not for that reason become validated as truth. The fact that millions of "satisfied" Muslims and Christians exist with mutually exclusive faith claims proves that a million satisfied customers *can* be wrong! Clearly times are now at hand when the masses are aligning themselves with *false* teachings over legitimate doctrines. However, unlike a custom-made hamburger, which is built for man's personal demands of consumption, doctrine is by definition something which belongs to its creator.

We live, however, with seemingly hopeless dependence on the marketplace for such validation. Even our theoretically democratic governmental systems are so designed that men get what they ultimately want (at least ideally) by voting for candidates who represent their desires. This culture has proven to be a fertile ground for the propagation of such false doctrines by the itchy ears of the crowd. The Word of Faith Movement has recognized and responded to the beacons of opportunity that exist in such soil.

They have made themselves exceptionally proficient at promising the desires of men's hearts. Every doctrinal position the movement holds is precisely crafted to appeal to the desires of a particular constituency. They have condescended themselves to the lowest possible rung of religiosity by claiming essentially what is touted by Satanism: that man can be like God, having the world in his own possession. Without the necessities of focus group studies, these men promise the desires of man *in spite* of what they happen to be. Indeed, any market of personal desire that develops will soon find a Word of Faith teacher prepared to instruct mankind (for the price of admission) on how to use "faith words" to receive it. Rest assured, "Speak Your Body Thin" and "Command Yourself to Beauty" are soon to follow, as these men are masters at scratching our cultural itches.

In the end, this counterfeit systematic theology puts man *literally* in the driver's seat of his life, being equal with God himself in ability to create his own universe. After all, in such a self-propelled system, what purpose remains for God? Returning to the original sin of Satan himself, WoF teachers have recognized and capitalized on the greatest itch man has ever had; his desire to be his own

Chapter 14 - The Biblical Response

god. Their demonic dogma aligns loyal followers with Satan himself as they ascribe to "be like the Most High." According to Hinn,

> "Let's say, I am a god man." This spirit man within me is a god-man. I'm a god-man."[130]

And Copeland concurs,

> "You don't have a god in you, you are one"[131]

> "I say this with all respect so that it don't upset you too bad, but I say it anyway. When I read in the Bible where he [Jesus] says, 'I Am,' I just smile and say, 'Yes, I Am, too!'"[132]

Itch, be scratched.

When I first began investigating the incredulous doctrines of this group, I must admit that I didn't initially comprehend the depths of their depravity. I thought Word of Faith preachers were run-of-the-mill tares in the wheat; flamboyant, misguided and half-baked theologians who got way too much attention. I've learned that they are much more. They are master deceivers who know what men want to hear and who have the skill to package, market and sell it week after week. They are opportunists who gladly contort God's eternal Word to suit the self-indulgence of their followers, which in turn feeds their own greed through donations and book sales that belong

---

[130] **Benny Hinn** (Praise the Lord, TBN, December 6, 1990)

[131] **Kenneth Copeland** (The Force of Love, 1987, audiotape #02-0028, side 1)

[132] **Kenneth Copeland** (Believer's Voice of Victory, TBN July 9, 1987)

in the fiction section of the library. They are the systematic fulfillment of scripture; those who men gather around themselves to, *"not serve our Lord Christ, but their own appetites, and by smooth talk and flattery they deceive the hearts of the naive."*[133]

Paul's wisdom, inspired by the Holy Spirit, should cause all who fear God and respect his Word to denounce loudly all such foolishness. He could no more clearly have stated what is obviously at large in today's open-minded theological soup of the WoF movement. *"The time is coming when people will not endure sound teaching."*

The term translated for "sound" (teaching) is the Gk. *hygiaino,* which literally means "healthy" or figuratively means "uncorrupted." How pertinent this term is to those who desire the honest truth of the scriptures. Being "uncorrupted" is precisely the antithesis of *apostasia,* as was observed in Chapter One. That which is apostate is that which was at one point rightly professed, but has since been rendered *unhealthy* and corrupted. The ears of those who formerly heard the truth are turned aside. They *know and have formerly embraced* good doctrine but choose to no longer endure it in light of more self-serving choices.

Simply put, to be a Word of Faith follower is to choose to abandon the scriptures altogether for something else. Scripture had these men and women pegged two thousand years ago. How foolish is he who takes the word of Benny Hinn, Copeland, Meyer and the growing number of cult leaders who have touted the fantasy doctrines of the WoF over the words of Jesus, Matthew, Peter, and Paul. These men lived in poverty. They were abused, beaten and ultimately killed for their faith. They never

---

[133] Romans 16:18

had mansions, maid services or million dollar wardrobes and they certainly would not have had half-billion dollar jets, had they been available. They gave their lives for a costly and despised truth, while today's false teacher prostitutes himself to Satan for the luxuries of this life. Paul asserts that,

> **2 Corinthians 11:13-15 (ESV)**
> [13] ... such men are false apostles, deceitful workmen, disguising themselves as apostles of Christ.
> [14] And no wonder, for even Satan disguises himself as an angel of light.
> [15] So it is no surprise if his servants, also, disguise themselves as servants of righteousness. Their end will correspond to their deeds.

My sincere hope is that the reader of this work will not be condemned along with them. The Word of God will save you from error, teach you the truth and guide you into spiritual maturity when left to its own testimony. To the apostate religious rulers of his own day, Jesus noted,

> **Matthew 22:29 (ESV)**
> [29] ... "You are wrong, because you know neither the Scriptures nor the power of God."

May this not be the verdict when *you* stand before him!

May your response to this colossal shift away from legitimate doctrine be to trust the Word of God as your only standard of faith and practice. I have not woven scripture throughout this work for the purposes of merely proving a point to the contrary. I have answered heresy with scripture because that is what Christians do: we trust the Word of God as our sole touchstone of faith and allow nothing else to intervene with its truths.

There is an old story about a man who set his watch every day by the grandfather clock in a jewelry store window.

As he passed by on his way to work he would check the clock faithfully to ensure he had the correct time. This was important to the man because his job, among other things, was to ring the whistle at the plant in town, signaling the beginning and end of the day's shift. One morning the owner of the jewelry store was sweeping outside as the man stopped for his regular time-check. The jeweler had become used to the man setting his clock each morning. He took great pride in the fact that this man daily trusted the impeccable grandfather clock as his time standard. He stated, "You must have a very important job to set your watch every morning by this clock." "I do," said the man. "I ring the whistle at the plant at 8 and 5 every day. I've always trusted your clock to keep me on time." Looking a bit sheepish, the jeweler confessed, "That's ironic…because I set that clock every day by *your plant whistle!*"

And therein lies the problem with trusting an improper standard. It leads to replicate errors. When we depend on other fallible human beings – especially those with an agenda – for our spiritual truth we will necessarily get off track sooner or later. If man leads man, with no outside standard, he tends to influence others who will in turn influence him. If a standard is not truly objective it will by nature bend and turn to the aspirations of the one who wields it. This is how the Word of Faith doctrine has apostatized: they have depended on new revelation that is outside of an objective standard. Such self-diagnosed testimonies of revelation have since influenced others, who in turn embraced the false doctrines of another man. Now, two men are teaching the same false doctrine, followed by four more. Such repetition of a common sentiment lends a perceived credibility to a flawed and untrustworthy premise. It is an utterly dishonest criterion to presume the self-confessed personal revelation of dreamers as a basis of one's faith. It is a wide road which leads to certain destruction.

Paul instructed Timothy concerning a very different course for believers in Christ:

> **2 Timothy 3:16-17 (ESV)**
> [16] *All Scripture is breathed out by God and profitable for teaching, for reproof, for correction, and for training in righteousness,*
> [17] *that the man of God may be competent, equipped for every good work.*

That scripture is "breathed out by God" is an exceptionally clear translation of this text. The Greek term *theopneustos* is a compound of *theos,* or God, and *pneo,* meaning breath, or air. Literally, the text exclaims that the Bible is God-breathed. If you want revelation concerning God, Christ, salvation and redemption, do not turn to a man's dreams and visions. Turn to God's breathed-out Word. It is profitable for teaching, for reproof, for correction, and for training in righteousness. This Word is the singular trustworthy standard of our faith which comes directly from God's own testimony. No other doctrinal source has ever remained firm.

If a man set out to sea on a long journey he would require a standard that would guide him to his destination. That standard may likely be a marine compass. If, however, his standard is off – even by a single degree – he will never reach his destination. Every mile that he travels will in fact lead him *further away* from his original course. One's standard must be absolutely trustworthy and utterly inerrant to be worthy of such a journey.

Why would one trust life's eternal journey to the testimony of a self-appointed religious teacher who claims to speak the truth when in fact his testimony follows a course contrary to one's own dependable compass of scripture? Such is the nature of the Word of Faith dogma and the result of apostasy. Many are those who have said, "This teaching is only off by small degrees here and there" and have continued to follow the course. Many are those who went so far as to marvel at the sights and sounds of the new course. They have cheered the boldness and flair of the new direction, admired the uncommon sights and paid pirate captains to lead contrarily to their formerly established criterion; a fully functioning and true compass.

The only course for a true believer in Christ to follow is the uncompromised Word of God. It is for this reason the gospel message has endured the past two thousand years. When the church got off track, which it certainly did, men were able to turn to God's Word which was affirmed first by Christ himself, and then by those whom he personally ordained to lead the church in the apostolic age. This God-breathed truth will lead you to God's answers for what you seek rather than man's. I will trust no man in any age who preaches contrary to that standard.

I implore you to do the same. God's word will save you from heresy. God's word will lead you from poverty, for he promises to those who place their faith in his gospel an eternal dwelling so rich that the streets are paved with translucent gold. It is God's word that will lead you to health, for in that same city of gold there is eternal health invested in a glorified body that can never perish. I have no doubt that those who are in pursuit of material wealth, health, glory and godhood will continue to gather around the Word-Faith message. But if your desire is for true spiritual regeneration and eternal glory, the WoF doctrine has nothing to offer you. Its teaching is devoid of a right gospel.

Conclusion

This book is actually quite concise on the subject of Word-Faith apostasy. There is much more that could be observed, but I have chosen to focus on the heavy hitters in the movement. Yet, there is an entire "Kansas City Prophet" movement which proclaims that God is speaking new truths continually through their falsified visions. There is a movement of absolutely incomprehensible worship practices featuring bizarre animal noises and frantic, spasmic writhing reminiscent of *The Exorcist* movies. There are men who literally beat their parishioners on stage; others who smoke imaginary marijuana joints, act stoned, and claim they're "tokin on Jesus." All of these inexplicable and unbiblical manifestations find their roots in this very same condemned Word of Faith movement. Once off track from the Scriptures, there is no limit to the bedlam that can be produced by any such movement.

Sadly, there are many who would agree that such manifestations are not of God and are unbiblical. Yet, they increasingly are being taken further down the road toward such chaos in their own local churches. In increasing measure, local congregations are breathing in the fanciful testimonies of the Word-Faith corruption. I hear music deejays on one of our local Christian radio stations speaking positive confessions over their circumstances on the air. I hear pastors of median sized local churches who preach concerning God's "promises" for his children to be financially prosperous. I had a personal friend several years ago who scolded me for acknowledging that I had a headache for fear that I would "speak condemnation" on myself and prolong my condition. Few have mansions or corporate jets, but many are buying into the same shell game that was originally authored and distributed by the false shepherds referred to in this work.

Make no mistake: if you follow these men, you are headed to the same condemnation as they are. Nor will there be any variance granted by our righteous judge for those who chose to believe such impostors over God's own written word.

In the end, sadly, if reading God's Word in light of the testimony of the WoF given thus far is not enough to dissuade one from following such foolish and perishing teachers, nothing will. God's plan has always been the presentation of the truth of Scripture as the means by which the Holy Spirit convicts and turns people from sin to salvation. It is the truth of a biblical gospel that sets men free. When that truth is rejected, men necessarily continue in the bondage of sin.

Thus, in conclusion of this work it is compulsory that a true and biblical message of atonement be preached, for through faith in this gospel comes freedom. The Holy Spirit indwells those he calls to such freedom and illuminates the truths of scripture to his chosen. If one hears and responds to the true gospel, ability to comprehend the deeper truths of scripture is thus illuminated; for he has journeyed at that point from darkness to light and from death to life.

One might think from a WoF perspective that salvation is a means to physical healing, financial empowerment or personal exaltation. Indeed, salvation brings such fulfillment – in every way – in its due time; for salvation leads to eternal life where there are no financial burdens, the body is resurrected and perfected forever and we are exalted in glory to honor Christ for all eternity. But, such things are only promised to believers within the context of an incorruptible and eternal existence. While Christ may indeed choose to free one from sickness or financial bondage, such things are not the substance of spiritual regeneration. It is sin that one is saved from in the biblical gospel. It is sin that is man's offense requiring Christ's blood as payment. It is sin that we are healed from immediately with the application of Christ's redemptive grace.

The scriptures proclaim from the very beginning that what God created was good, right and unblemished by sin.[134] At that time, God revealed to man but one simple law:

> **Genesis 2:16-17 (ESV)**
> *[16] And the LORD God commanded the man, saying, "You may surely eat of every tree of the garden,*
> *[17] but of the tree of the knowledge of good and evil you shall not eat, for in the day that you eat of it you shall surely die."*

Forget all of the WoF nonsense about Adam being a little god. If he were, he could not have been tempted to *become like* God. He was simply a man whom God had formed to reveal his glory through. In the establishment of his superiority in all things, the Lord granted that one simple law. And, for the breaking of this law God prescribed a very simple, but costly penalty. If Adam and Eve ate the forbidden fruit, they would die.

Adam and Eve had every good food at their disposal. They had no legitimate reason to stray from God's ordained command. But they were tempted by the original sinner, Satan, and disobeyed God's command.

---

[134] Genesis 1:31

> **Genesis 3:1-6 (ESV)**
> *¹ Now the serpent was more crafty than any other beast of the field that the LORD God had made. He said to the woman, "Did God actually say, 'You shall not eat of any tree in the garden'?"*
> *² And the woman said to the serpent, "We may eat of the fruit of the trees in the garden,*
> *³ but God said, 'You shall not eat of the fruit of the tree that is in the midst of the garden, neither shall you touch it, lest you die.'"*
> *⁴ But the serpent said to the woman, "You will not surely die.*
> *⁵ For God knows that when you eat of it your eyes will be opened, and you will be like God, knowing good and evil."*
> *⁶ So when the woman saw that the tree was good for food, and that it was a delight to the eyes, and that the tree was to be desired to make one wise, she took of its fruit and ate, and she also gave some to her husband who was with her, and he ate.*

Thus, sin entered the world. The Bible explains that through Adam's breaking of God's law every person that followed from his line would be born into sin.

> **Romans 5:12 (ESV)**
> *¹² Therefore, just as sin came into the world through one man, and death through sin, and so death spread to all men because all sinned—*

Paul asserts that death followed sin, just as God had noted it would. Death was physical and spiritual. Physically we all die, in spite of the affirmations of WoF preachers. There is no one who skirts this curse. One must wonder why WoF preachers are buried every year if, indeed, they need only to confess positive words to maintain perfect health. The modern father of the movement, Ken Hagin, who once claimed to have never had a headache, himself succumbed to death as the result a heart condition. He could not profess his illness away; it was God's prescribed penalty of death that finds us all through our weakened and judged bodies. Copeland, Hinn, Osteen and every other WoF preacher will perish from this life just as surely. Physical death is God's sentence for sin. It cannot be avoided by sinful man except that the Lord return and redeem those who remain living; instantly transforming them into their eternal stead.

Make no mistake: Christ *did indeed* provide for the penalty of physical death in his atonement. We are surely promised to be freed from physical illness and death via a future resurrection. Yet, Paul makes it inescapably clear that the resurrection to eternal life is a future event which leads one from this fallen material world into an uncontaminated world in eternity. Paul stated definitively,

> *1 Corinthians 15:20-22 (ESV)*
> [20] *But in fact Christ has been raised from the dead, the firstfruits of those who have fallen asleep.*
> [21] *For as by a man came death, by a man has come also the resurrection of the dead.*
> [22] *For as in Adam all die, so also in Christ shall all be made alive.*

However, Paul makes no acquittal for the judged and dying physical body prior to death. The penalty of physical death will remain squarely upon us until our moment of freedom, which comes *because of our death* and departure from this earth. As Paul states earlier in this chapter,

> *1 Corinthians 15:35-36 (ESV)*
> [35] *But someone will ask, "How are the dead raised? With what kind of body do they come?"*
> [36] *You foolish person! What you sow does not come to life unless it dies.*

Thus, the judged body *must* succumb to death in order to be regenerated into a glorious new body. This is not to say that God may not give us a temporary reprieve of some of the symptoms of death. He may in fact heal one of his beloved from an earthly illness. But, the true culprit from which all earthly illness arises is the judgment of death levied against our sinful bodies. It is impossible for us to enter Heaven in our judged bodies. We must die, or be transfigured by the return of Christ, before we can experience the fullness of our healing via a renewed, imperishable body. He notes in verse 50,

> **1 Corinthians 15:50 (ESV)**
> *^{50} I tell you this, brothers: flesh and blood cannot inherit the kingdom of God, nor does the perishable inherit the imperishable.*

Physical deterioration and death are God's own penalty. There is no "Word-Faith" that can undo what God has done. He did not say "you might die," but "you will surely die." Likewise, Romans informs us that,

> **Romans 6:23 (ESV)**
> *^{23} ... the wages of sin is death, but the free gift of God is eternal life in Christ Jesus our Lord.*

Because of Adam's sin, as Romans 5:12 noted, we all have become guilty. Every person that reads this work is guilty of sin.[135] No one ever taught us how to sin; we were simply born with a fully functioning sin nature. Every toddler knows how to lie, cheat and throw a walleyed tantrum. Grandma didn't teach them such disobedience while mom and dad weren't looking. They didn't learn it from watching violent cartoons. Sin is simply inherent in the human condition. And, for every person who sins, God's law remains – complete with the original penalty intact.

---

[135] Ephesians 2:1-2

Sin's penalty is also spiritual. By default, no one will receive the glorious body described above. Because we were born into sin we were also born into the full judgment of sin which is physical and spiritual death. Jesus said,

> **Matthew 13:40-42 (ESV)**
> [40] *Just as the weeds are gathered and burned with fire, so will it be at the close of the age.*
> [41] *The Son of Man will send his angels, and they will gather out of his kingdom all causes of sin and all law-breakers,*
> [42] *and throw them into the fiery furnace. In that place there will be weeping and gnashing of teeth.*

"All law-breakers" refers to every one of us in our inherited sinful state. We all break God's laws daily and are sentenced by default for an eternal destruction in a lake of fire. No passage of scripture depicts this more clearly than Revelation 21.

> **Revelation 21:8 (ESV)**
> [8] *But as for the cowardly, the faithless, the detestable, as for murderers, the sexually immoral, sorcerers, idolaters, and all liars, their portion will be in the lake that burns with fire and sulfur, which is the second death."*

Specifically noting "the second death," it is crystal clear that God's judgment for sin is eternal, not merely temporal. Likewise, chapter 20 of that book notes,

> **Revelation 20:14-15 (ESV)**
> [14] *Then Death and Hades were thrown into the lake of fire. This is the second death, the lake of fire.*
> [15] *And if anyone's name was not found written in the book of life, he was thrown into the lake of fire.*

Anyone whose name was not found in the "book of life" is to be cast into the eternal place of torment. The penalty for sin for us today is precisely what it has always been.

Death is in store for each of us physically and spiritually. Rest assured, however, that there is hope for redemption in Christ. One is not relegated to this torment if one receives by faith the true Gospel of Christ. But death is the congenital status of every sinner according to God's law.

At his chosen time God revealed more of his law to Moses.[136] Overall he revealed some 613 commands in the Old Testament. These commands included both the definitions of sin and its penalty. Never was there a man who could keep God's law fully until Christ. And, never has there been a man who could keep God's law since. Man is sinful at his core and he continually failed throughout the testimony of scripture and history.

God is a just God.[137] As a righteous judge, he cannot simply overlook man's sin. He prescribed the penalty for sin with full resolve to carry it out as our judge. A good judge cannot overlook an infraction of the law, even if it comes at the hand of his own loved ones. A good judge – a just judge – will observe the law and its penalty for the sake of justice; that right and wrong remain clearly defined and that the penal consequences required are exacted upon those who deserve it. In light of God's law and his eternal righteous character, you and I deserve the physical and eternal consequence of death. And, in spite of the shallow words of some today, God will follow through on such sentencing; because he is just.

But, the good news is that God is also gracious.[138] Grace is simply and rightly defined as "God's unmerited favor."

---

[136] Exodus 34:28

[137] Romans 3:25-26

[138] Ephesians 2:5-8

We have no reason for God to be good to us for we have broken his law and live as his enemies.[139] We are law-breakers who live before the law-giver as guilty and condemned. But God demonstrated favor on us that we did not deserve. God's grace was revealed clearly through the same Old Testament law given to Moses. God provided that the death sentence for man's sins could be demanded of a properly applied blood sacrifice.

> ***Leviticus 17:11 (ESV)***
> *[11] For the life of the flesh is in the blood, and I have given it for you on the altar to make atonement for your souls, for it is the blood that makes atonement by the life.*

It was God's gracious gift to ancient man that his sins could be covered by the vicarious blood of an animal sacrifice. Death was required as the penalty for sin, and death was granted through the blood of a substitutionary animal. This sacrificial system was a daily reality in ancient Israel. Every day there were morning and evening sacrifices. There were Sabbath and New Moon sacrifices. There were a multitude of sacrifices required for Israel's holy days. The tabernacles and temples were accordingly designed to accommodate the offering of blood sacrifices. There was an altar upon which the blood of such animals was sprinkled and their flesh consumed by fire in order to offer a continual offering to the Lord.

In the very center of the Temple was an inner room called "the Holy of Holies." It was in this location that God's Name dwelt. Only the high priest could enter the Holy of Holies, and then, only on one particular day each year: Yom Kippur. *Yom Kippur* is Hebrew for "the day of atonement." It was a day that provided a yearly offering

---

[139] Romans 5:10

of blood to exact justice upon the sins of the people. At Yom Kippur the high priest would sacrifice a bull for his own sins and a goat for the sins of the people. He would apply that blood directly before God's presence in the Holy of Holies. It is this act of providing blood for atonement that Jesus Christ fulfilled by his death on a cross.

The sacrifices required by God's law were offered repetitively, but the blood of Christ was presented once and for all. The author of Hebrews notes,

> **Hebrews 10:11-14 (ESV)**
> *[11] And every priest stands daily at his service, offering repeatedly the same sacrifices, which can never take away sins.*
> *[12] But when Christ had offered for all time a single sacrifice for sins, he sat down at the right hand of God,*
> *[13] waiting from that time until his enemies should be made a footstool for his feet.*
> *[14] For by a single offering he has perfected for all time those who are being sanctified.*

The blood of the old covenant never took sins away; it merely covered them until the next sacrifice was offered. But Christ shed his blood for an eternal, irrevocable covenant through which every sin of every man that trusted in Christ's provision could be permanently forgiven. Please understand that it was not some mystical and unbiblical "punishment in Hell" by which Christ paid for the sins of the world. It was the spilling of Christ's own perfect blood for the sake of sinful man. Jesus fulfilled the roles of both high priest and sacrifice by offering himself on a greater altar than that of the temple. He offered Himself directly to God as the blood payment required to fulfill the law.

> **Hebrews 9:11-14 (ESV)**
> *[11] But when Christ appeared as a high priest of the*

> *good things that have come, then through the greater and more perfect tent (not made with hands, that is, not of this creation)*
> *[12] he entered once for all into the holy places, not by means of the blood of goats and calves but by means of his own blood, thus securing an eternal redemption.*
> *[13] For if the blood of goats and bulls, and the sprinkling of defiled persons with the ashes of a heifer, sanctify for the purification of the flesh,*
> *[14] how much more will the blood of Christ, who through the eternal Spirit offered himself without blemish to God, purify our conscience from dead works to serve the living God.*

Many have heard the sentiment that "Jesus died for you," or that "Jesus died for sins." Few truly understand the miracle of atonement in Christ: it was a fulfillment of all that God had ever said concerning sin, death and atonement. Jesus' own words were,

> **Matthew 5:17 (ESV)**
> *[17] "Do not think that I have come to abolish the Law or the Prophets; I have not come to abolish them but to fulfill them.*

And fulfill the law he did. God's grace has always been granted vicariously through blood offering. Death is the eternal penalty of sin and thus death is required by God's justice or forgiveness simply cannot be obtained. His act of grace, however, was the allowing of a substitution; originally in the animal sacrificial system and finally in the provision of the blood of His own Son. Contrary to what Copeland, Hinn, Meyer and a myriad of WoF teachers propose, the Bible proclaims loudly and clearly that it was the physical shed blood of Christ that bought redemption for mankind.

> **Colossians 1:19-20 (ESV)**
> *[19] For in him all the fullness of God was pleased to dwell,*

> [20] *and through him to reconcile to himself all things, whether on earth or in heaven, making peace by the blood of his cross.*

Thus, God's substitutionary system of blood sacrifice for the remission of sins was completed by Christ's physical bloodshed on the cross. Christ furthermore demonstrated his authority over death by being resurrected from the grave. His resurrection proved the acceptability of his sacrificial death before God. He thus became the forerunner of all believers; having died and been resurrected to the glorified body which can never die again. Through his death the debt for sin was paid. Through his resurrection he proved his sufficiency as our substitute. The good news of Christ is that we can be forgiven by hearing this biblical gospel message, placing our faith in him and trusting Christ alone for our redemption.

As to the application of Christ's work on the cross, it is obtained by faith in this gospel message. One is not saved by statically knowing this gospel, but by grace through faith.

> **Ephesians 2:8-9 (ESV)**
> [8] *For by grace you have been saved through faith. And this is not your own doing; it is the gift of God,*
> [9] *not a result of works, so that no one may boast.*

Grace is revealed by God in the application of Christ's atonement. It is only by grace that Christ came, fulfilled the law, died a substitutionary death and was resurrected. We did not deserve His work, but receive it solely by the Grace of Him who provided it. No one is saved from death to life for living a good life, or being shrewd enough to pounce on Christ's provision. The very act of believing and receiving this message is itself a work of

God's grace, for God alone can bring one to saving faith in Christ.[140] Peter's confession of Christ, which Jesus identified as the foundational confession of the church, was itself noted by Christ to be something that God had revealed to him. When asked, "who do you say that I am" by Christ, Peter noted,

> **Matthew 16:16-17 (ESV)**
> [16] ... *"You are the Christ, the Son of the living God."*
> [17] *And Jesus answered him, "Blessed are you, Simon Bar-Jonah! For flesh and blood has not revealed this to you, but my Father who is in heaven.*

When one hears this gospel of Christ and believes, they are doing so by the very work of God Himself; having revealed the truth of the gospel message to the hearer. This is – and has always been – the modus operandi of the gospel. The gospel is preached, God allows men to hear and faith is born. As Paul states it,

> **Romans 10:17 (ESV)**
> [17] *So faith comes from hearing, and hearing through the word of Christ.*

Faith is the motivational catalyst of the gospel. No one is saved without faith, as Ephesians 2:8 notes, "for by grace you have been saved through faith." A foundational element of faith is that one believes the message they have heard of Christ's atoning work: that Christ is God come to earth and sacrificed for sin. But, James notes,

> **James 2:19 (ESV)**
> [19] *You believe that God is one; you do well. Even the demons believe—and shudder!*

Thus, faith does not represent merely a cognitive understanding of the technical details of the gospel. Faith

---

[140] John 6:44

is responsive in its nature. Because one truly and wholly believes he is thus motivated to receive and trust that truth for his salvation. Faith is not the empty shell that WoF preachers claim it is. Faith is not a "powerful force" that exists parallel to God. It is not the means by which we "command our world" to do this or that. Faith has God as its object. Saving faith is illustrated by one's response to hearing the truth. It is an active commitment to the truth that one has believed. As such, a byproduct of faith is repentance, or a change of mind. When one hears the gospel message of Christ, faith produces repentance so that the hearer turns to trust Christ for his salvation and turns thus away from his former life of self-sufficiency and sin. In Acts, Paul speaks of

> **Acts 20:21 (ESV)**
> *[21] testifying both to Jews and to Greeks of repentance toward God and of faith in our Lord Jesus Christ.*

Repentance, as the product of faith, leads one to know full well that Jesus Christ is God, Lord and Savior of their lives over sin. As such, one does not come to Christ for the free gift of salvation without a full and knowing acquiescence of His deity and rule. Mere "belief" *can be* simply a static affirmation without life change. Faith is neither static nor lacking in repentance; it urges the believer to unconditionally trust in Christ alone as the guarantor of salvation.

Paul testified to King Agrippa in Acts concerning his call from Christ. He noted the words of Christ calling him to preach the gospel,

> **Acts 26:18-20 (ESV)**
> *[18] to open their eyes, so that they may turn from darkness to light and from the power of Satan to God, that they may receive forgiveness of sins and a place among those who are sanctified by faith in me.'*

Paul continues,

> [19] "Therefore, O King Agrippa, I was not disobedient to the heavenly vision,
> [20] but declared first to those in Damascus, then in Jerusalem and throughout all the region of Judea, and also to the Gentiles, that they should repent and turn to God, performing deeds in keeping with their repentance.

Thus, repentance is turning to God and engaging a new life in Christ "in keeping with their repentance."

The gospel call is a call to believe the written word of God. It is a call to understand that Christ fulfilled the law by offering Himself as the final, unmitigated payment for sins. It is faith which leads to repentance; turning from your former life of sin and death to Christ's forgiveness and a life of service to Him as Lord and King. This *does not mean* that one "earns" their salvation by doing the right types of service. Such is impossible. Salvation is granted by grace solely through God's work. But it is one's response to Christ in faith which produces repentance leading to the service of Christ.

I implore the readers of this work to shun the falsified man-centric gospel of the WoF movement and receive the true and unwavering gospel of Christ as revealed in the scriptures. Count yourself blessed to suffer through whatever your King prescribes in this life with patient endurance, knowing that a future everlasting restoration from the wages of sin awaits the redeemed.

The most tragic and eternally destructive failure of the Word of Faith message is its utterly consumerized approach to salvation. This platform relegates the greatest news the world has ever heard to insignificance by purporting that salvation is about money, health and power over the petty circumstances of this fleeting life. These things have absolutely no value in light of being forgiven for sin and ensured an eternal restoration to our creator. Such an understanding is not that of one who has truly known Christ. Paul, who sacrificed excessively in his temporal life, proclaimed,

> **Philippians 3:8-11 (ESV)**
> [8] *Indeed, I count everything as loss because of the surpassing worth of knowing Christ Jesus my Lord. For his sake I have suffered the loss of all things and count them as rubbish, in order that I may gain Christ* [9] *and be found in him, not having a righteousness of my own that comes from the law, but that which comes through faith in Christ, the righteousness from God that depends on faith—*
> [10] *that I may know him and the power of his resurrection, and may share his sufferings, becoming like him in his death,*
> [11] *that by any means possible I may attain the resurrection from the dead.*

The Word of Faith program is a lie. It is fruitless. It is powerless. It cannot redeem your soul from eternal destruction. Even if its principles worked – which they do not – it is devoid of the true gospel of scripture.

The trustworthy gospel of scripture is not a means to your best life now, but eternally. It is the truth of God that Christ offers redemption and restoration to those who by faith receive it.

> **Philippians 3:18-21 (ESV)**
> [18] *For many, of whom I have often told you and now tell you even with tears, walk as enemies of the cross of Christ.*
> [19] *Their end is destruction, their god is their belly, and they glory in their shame, with minds set on earthly things.*
> [20] *But our citizenship is in heaven, and from it we await a Savior, the Lord Jesus Christ,*
> [21] *who will transform our lowly body to be like his*

glorious body, by the power that enables him even to subject all things to himself.

Scripture Reference

(Page Numbers Approximate)

Genesis
1:26, p. 72
1:31, p. 211
2:16–17, p. 211
2:17, p. 112
3, p. 74
3:1, p. 29
3:1–6, p. 212
3:15, p. 139
3:17, p. 82
3:23–24, p. 85
4:7, p. 112
6, p. 81
12:7, p. 139
20:17, p. 152
32:30, 33:20, p. 49

Exodus
21:32, p. 182
34:28, p. 216

Leviticus
12:7–8, p. 183
17:11, p. 217

Deuteronomy
10:14, p. 82
18:22, p. 54
24:3, p. 7
32:39, p. 90

1 Samuel
16:13, p. 101

1 Chronicles
29:11, p. 90

Job
9:12, p. 91
23:13, p. 83
25:2, p. 91
41:11, p. 91

Psalms
2, p. 139
8:5, p. 73
8:5–8, p. 74
16, pp. 116, 118
16:10, pp. 118, 120
18:30, p. 54
22, p. 139
22:18, p. 179
24:1, p. 82
33:11, p. 83
83:17–18, p. 92
100:3, p. 78
105:15, p. 16
139, p. 119
139:8, p. 119
139:15–16, p. 78

Proverbs
10:4, p. 194
19:21, p. 83

224 | Scripture Reference

Isaiah
9:6, pp. 96, 108
14:12–14, p. 77
14:14, p. 92
40:8, p. 45
41:4, p. 60
42:8, p. 78
43:10, p. 78
45:21, p. 78
50:1, p. 7
53, pp. 140, 150, 151, 152, 153, 155, 156
53:4–6, p. 150
53:5, pp. 139, 153, 154, 156
53:6, p. 154
53:11, p. 114
53:12, pp. 114, 155
61, p. 189

Jeremiah
3:8, p. 7
14:14, pp. 18, 32, 33, 83
14:14–16, p. 17
19:11, p. 152
23:5–6, p. 96
23:26, p. 18
29:8, p. 18

Ezekiel
47:8, p. 152

Hosea
13:14, p. 118

Malachi
1:8, p. 133

Matthew
1:23, p. 96
4:18–20, p. 185
4:21–22, p. 185
5:17, pp. 112, 219
5:31, p. 7
8:16–17, p. 151
8:19–20, p. 177
12, p. 114
12:23, p. 115
12:24, p. 115
12:27–31, p. 115
13:40–42, p. 215
16:16–17, p. 221
16:21, p. 184
17:22–23, p. 184
18:8, p. 158
19:7, p. 7
20:18–19, p. 184
22:29, pp. 44, 203
24:10–11, p. 11
25, p. 125
25:26–27, p. 194
25:41, pp. 121, 125
26:14–15, p. 181
27:3–10, p. 181
27:57–60, p. 183

Mark
5:7–10, p. 135
10:4, p. 7

Luke
1:32–33, p. 139
2:22–24, p. 183
4:18, pp. 188, 189
4:33–34, p. 134
4:38, p. 178
18:24–25, p. 191
21:33, p. 53

Apostasy! | 225

John
1, pp. 64, 65, 76, 145, 176
1:1–3, p. 64
1:10, p. 107
1:12–13, p. 145
1:14, pp. 65, 107
1:35–39, p. 176
3, p. 144
3:1–6, p. 144
4:24, p. 50
6:44, p. 221
8:44, p. 32
10, p. 99
10:24–30, p. 98
10:31–33, p. 99
12:1, p. 178
19, p. 178
19:23–24, p. 179
20:27–28, p. 96

Acts
4:11–12, p. 138
13:6, p. 21
15:7, p. 189
18:1–3, p. 187
20:21, p. 222
20:28, p. 96
20:29–30, p. 28
26:18–20, p. 222

Romans
3:22, p. 39
3:25–26, p. 216
3:26, p. 96
4:16, p. 39
5:10, p. 217
5:12, pp. 212, 214
6:23, pp. 112, 214
8, p. 142
8:29, p. 142
9:6, p. 96
10:17, pp. 47, 221
12:1, p. 172
14, p. 21
14:1, p. 22
16:17–18, pp. 29, 147
16:18, p. 202

1 Corinthians
1:17–18, p. 123
4:10–12, p. 187
9:1–18, p. 187
10:26, p. 82
15, p. 105
15:20–22, p. 213
15:35–36, p. 213
15:42–49, p. 105
15:50, p. 214
15:50–53, pp. 141, 158

2 Corinthians
2:17, p. 30
5:21, pp. 110, 112
8:2, p. 174
11:4, p. 34
11:13–15, pp. 18, 34, 203
12:7–10, p. 166

Galatians
1:6–8, p. 45
2:14, p. 190
4:17, p. 28

Ephesians
2:1–2, p. 214
2:5–8, p. 216
2:8, pp. 39, 221
2:8–9, p. 220

4:7–9, p. 119
4:28, p. 193

Philippians
1:15, p. 28
2, pp. 103, 104
2:5–8, p. 103
3:8–11, p. 224
3:18–21, p. 224
4:12, p. 174

Colossians
1:18, p. 140
1:19–20, pp. 123, 219
2:8, p. 31
2:9, pp. 104, 108
2:13–15, p. 135

1 Thessalonians
5:2, p. 9

2 Thessalonians
2:1–3, p. 9

1 Timothy
1:3–4, p. 20
4:1, pp. 10, 33
4:1–6, p. 18
6:3–4, p. 18
6:3–5, pp. 29, 173
6:6–11, p. 170
6:10, p. 30

2 Timothy
2:16–18, p. 21
3, p. 48
3:16–17, pp. 46, 205
4:3–4, pp. 3, 10, 198

Titus
1:10–14, p. 19
1:11, pp. 30, 168
1:16, p. 18

Hebrews
4:15, p. 133
9, p. 132
9:11–14, p. 218
9:14, p. 132
9–10, p. 132
10:1–14, p. 96
10:11–14, p. 218
11, pp. 56, 61
11:1, p. 55
11:3, p. 61
11:4, p. 56
11:17, p. 57

James
1:9–10, p. 190
1:17, p. 53
2:5–7, p. 191
2:19, pp. 57, 221

1 Peter
1:19, p. 133
1:23, p. 146
2:24, p. 156
2:25, p. 157
4:17, p. 189

2 Peter
2:17–19, p. 31

Jude
1:3–4, pp. 6, 15
1:4, p. 1

Revelation
2:9, p. 174
2:20, p. 21
3:1, p. 3
19:20, p. 125
20:1–9, p. 125
20:10, p. 125
20:11–15, p. 125
20:14, p. 121
20:14–15, p. 215
21, p. 215
21:4, p. 153
21:8, p. 215

CPSIA information can be obtained at www.ICGtesting.com
Printed in the USA
LVOW10s1821171113

361657LV00024B/535/P